Reiki Healing for Beginners

By

David Filipe

Copyright © 2019 David filipe

All rights reserved.

Dedication

To everyone who wants a better way to heal, and be healed.

Table of contents

Introduction..............................5

Chapter One reiki and christianity...13

Chapter Two reiki symbols and meanings..............................26

Chapter Three reiki hand positions..36

Chapter Four chakras....................59

Chapter Five the root chakra............63

Chapter Six the sacral chakra..........77

Chapter Seven the solar plexus chakra..................................90

Chapter Eight the heart chakra..........104

Chapter Nine the throat chakra..........118

Chapter Ten the third eye chakra.......131

Chapter Eleven the crown chakra...143

Chapter Twelve types of reiki systems...153

Chapter Thirteen_reiki aura................169

Chapter Fourteen_reiki and healing crystals...175

Chapter Fifteen space cleansing with reiki...186

Chapter Sixteen kundalini energy......194

CONCLUSION.......................................198

Introduction

First thing I thought to myself when I heard 'Reiki' for the first time was **"Holy fudge! What?!"** I get it. I totally do. Reiki isn't even English. It's a Japanese method for relaxation and healing.

Think... Japanese spa.

Just like a regular spa, Reiki involves body contact, sort of. In a typical Reiki session, the 'masseuse' will let his hands hover over your body close to your skin, but not quite touching it. While he/she does this, some energy shoots out of their palms - **no, you won't be able to see it** - into your body. I know it sounds unbelievable because you can't see this 'energy,' but you will be able to feel it.

Every living organism possesses energy, a kind of lifeforce. This energy is the reason why we are still alive and breathing and walking and feeling. And just like your smartphone, we need to recharge sometimes and Reiki is a great way to do that.

The word Reiki was coined from two Japanese terms. **Rei** which is God's wisdom or power and **Ki** which is lifeforce. So Reiki basically means Energy from God.

This energy is present in and around us, like a forcefield. It flows through every muscle, nerve and blood vessel. It is the very essence of your being. Reiki is involved in your physical wellbeing, that is your different organs and systems. It also affects your mental wellbeing, that is your thoughts and intelligence. It affects your emotional health too, and lastly, it is an important part of your spiritual health.

Reiki is pretty straightforward and easy to learn. It is an essential life skill because drugs can't fix everything. Did you know Reiki can fix that recurrent flu you have? Or your mom's backache? Although Reiki shouldn't be a substitute for medicine in certain cases, it can do some jobs just fine.

Learning Reiki has nothing to do with your IQ or spirituality, so pretty much anyone can use it. You don't need super high SAT scores to learn Reiki. A lot of people have successfully mastered the art of Reiki despite their age or origin. I know you're thinking, "Another religion?' No, Reiki isn't a religion despite all the spiritual stuff surrounding it. It is not a religion because you don't need to believe in a particular deity to learn and properly use Reiki.

A man named Mikao Usui discovered Reiki a long, long time ago. He taught that a person's thoughts, speech, and actions should promote peace and balance, and this idea is accepted by religions and cultures across the world.

Reiki is all about balance; emotionally, mentally, physically and spiritually. It is an art that has proven itself over generations by thousands of people. Reiki typically involves a practitioner and recipient. I'll explain how in a bit.

What Is Expected During A Reiki Session

When you go for your first Reiki session, there are certain things that will happen that shouldn't alarm you because it is part of the process, I assure you. You will be told to lie down on a bed, massage table or couch. You will be asked to remove your shoes. You may also be told to take off your belt or at least loosen it so that it isn't likely to affect your breathing during the session.

You may keep your clothes on during the session. It is better to wear loose clothing made from natural sources like wool or cotton when going for a Reiki appointment. You might also be told to take off any bracelet, ring, pendant, watch, and stuff like that before the session begins, so it's better to leave your jewellery in the jewellery box.

Relaxing Atmosphere

Some Reiki healers usually prepare the room before you arrive. You might notice some candles or scented flowers or bubbling fountains or relaxing songs when you arrive. It's all for you to feel comfortable. Some other healers prefer to work in a quiet environment. It all depends.

Healing Touch

After you're all relaxed and ready for the session, it begins. The healer will lay his hands over your body. His hands might be an inch or so away from your skin, but not quite touching it.

Some healers even follow a step-by-step method of hand placements because it makes sure they get their hands everywhere before the session is over. The empathic healers just move their hands to where they feel it is needed the most.

Some healers like hands-on contact, so they might actually touch you, but don't panic. It's part of the process. Honestly, it doesn't matter whether or not they touch you because the Reiki energy will flow to the part of your body that needs it the most.

Phantom Hands

During Reiki, there's this thing that you may or may not experience. It is called **phantom hands.** This happens because, as I said, Reiki goes to the areas where it is needed the most. Some people who have experienced phantom hands describe them as feeling the healer's hands on a part of your body, when in fact their hands are actually somewhere else. *Creepy, I know.*

For instance, you might feel hands on your feet when in fact the healer has his hands on your shoulders and sometimes you may feel more than a pair of hands on your body as if you're being worked on by more than one healer.

Difference Between Reiki and Healing Touch

Reiki and "healing touch" are somewhat similar forms of healing, but there are obvious differences between the two. They are both energy drugs and can be used to open chakras and heal physical illnesses. The way this works is through a process called channeling. The healer transfers their lifeforce into you and this helps kickstart the healing process. Sometimes you won't need to take pills if you're getting regular Reiki sessions.

Healing touch, unlike Reiki, doesn't require some kind of alignment of your own energy before you can practice it. Healing touch was founded by Janet R. N. Mentgen and was originally used by those in the medical field. But recently, anyone can practice it because we all have energy flowing through us. Any random person can learn healing touch in a single weekend. *Isn't that amazing?*

Healing Touch is also called therapeutic touch and involves knowing about the auras and chakras which will be discussed in further chapters. It is basically a method of making the body self-heal.

Reiki differs from healing touch; in that you need to be in complete alignment before you can use it to help heal others. In Reiki, lifeforce or energy known as **Qi** is transferred from the healer to the body of the recipient, and this energy goes on to heal the psyche, soul and body of the person. So if you're not in alignment, you won't be doing much good for them.

The same way a sick doctor can't fix up anyone, Reiki healers must be balanced before they can balance anyone. If the expert's **Qi** is blocked, you can bet that no energy is flowing anywhere. Usui Mikao trained more than two thousand students in the Reiki healing art before he passed on.

In Reiki, the healers hands won't touch your body

like in healing touch - that literally has the word "touch" in it. This no contact healing is preferred by most people who have a problem with physical contact. Like autistic people, for example.

So now that you know a little bit about what Reiki is, let's jump into the meat of it all!

Chapter One

REIKI AND CHRISTIANITY

Reiki is becoming more popular every day, and so many Christians have begun to show interest in this healing system. Some have even started practicing it. Christians have realized how useful Reiki is in showing compassion to other people. They have also benefited from the different forms of healing and how it draws them closer to God through a connection only them can explain. Reiki healing art is quite similar to what Jesus Christ did during his time on Earth because it involves laying of hands. This makes it particularly appealing to Christians.

Is It Okay for Christians to Practice Reiki?

There's a lot of confusion about Christianity and Reiki practice. So many Christians are drawn to the healing art of Reik, but do not know if it is okay to practice it because of their faith. Some even take months to think about whether or not they should visit a Reiki center. These people keep their interests in Reiki a secret because nobody wants to be criticized or burned at the stake or something. A young man once said that Christianity does not leave room for the healing art of Reiki, but he made up his mind to listen to the voice of God and accept the blessing that is Reiki. That young man was me.

Some people don't think highly of Reiki because of certain stories they have heard and whatnot. A young woman didn't buy into the idea of Reiki because she heard stories about a Reiki healer who abused his patients, but the crimes of one person should not apply to the whole. *I mean, humanity isn't all stupid because of a few dimwits, am I right?*

A Reiki Miracle

I know someone who had slipped and fallen on the hardwood floor when he was leaving a store. After trying all sorts of medication, he went straight to a Reiki gathering I was at, and told us what had happened. He was clearly in pain while he recounted his story. A few minutes later, I offered to give him Reiki. However, he felt a bit doubtful, but he decided to try it anyway. Prior to this devastating fall, he had already fallen once before, and had badly hurt the base of his spine. In other words, he was in a ridiculous amount of pain. After the session though, he felt amazing! He couldn't believe how well Reiki had worked for him.

Oddly enough he didn't call anymore or request more Reiki sessions. A while later, I got through to him and he told me he decided to research Reiki. He found out he didn't buy into the idea of a person transferring energy from their bodies to another person, and thought it was something he ought not to mess around with, because he had read some weird articles about Reiki and demons.

The truth is you can choose to look at Reiki from whatever perspective you want to. You can choose to gobble up ignorant stuff, or you can choose to learn about Reiki from the people who actually practice it and have a deep understanding of it. Your call.

Reiki has been quickly spreading around the world for over 39 years and people are slowly becoming open minded about it. Christians have also started accepting and using Reiki in so many ways. Christians are even more inclined to study Reiki because it helps them further understand how Jesus healed the sick during his time here on Earth. Others are worried Reiki has a different source and are researching it to prove their point. It's perfectly okay.

Usually, when there is a change in our reality, we try to study and process this new information and sometimes new information has a bearing on our religious ideologies and convictions. The people who are really in tune with their spirituality usually have no trouble understanding energy and working with it in their lives. This doesn't mean you're in the wrong for not choosing to adopt Reiki. I'm just saying if you need healing, or you know someone who does, then you're missing out!

As Christians look for new ways to grow on the spirit, many have accepted practices that help build up the "Endowments of the Soul." I'm not making this up. Go ahead and check out the book of 1st Corinthians, Chapter 12, and read from verses 4 to 12. Here, the apostle Paul talks about the blessings of the Holy Spirit, which include discernment, speaking in tongues, and the laying on of hands to heal the sick. Since one of the gifts of the Holy Spirit is healing, committed Christians who are focused on the teachings of the Bible have given some thought to Healing Touch and Reiki.

As a Christian, you might seriously be a more than a little bit worried about whether or not you should even be holding this book in the first place. But if you look through the Bible for guidance, you're going to discover you're getting worked up over nothing, my friend. See, even Jesus made use of Reiki **a lot.** How do you think he performed his healing miracles? Off the top of my head, I can think of several instances where he made use of Reiki.

1. Jesus used contact to heal a wealthy man's relative of a fever (Matthew 8:14-15)
2. Jesus used his hands to fix up a man with infection (Luke 5:12-13)
3. Jesus healed two blind men by just touching their eyes (Matthew 20:29-34)
4. Jesus raised the dead by laying his hands on her (Luke 8: 49-55)

Besides, sacred writing obviously states it is okay for a Christian to be a healer. Christians who have a strong faith in God believe that God will surely direct them. *Why not you too?*

Similarities Between Reiki and Christianity

I frequently come across Christians who are not ready to accept or practice Reiki on the grounds that they feel it is conflicting with Christianity and the lessons of Christ.

As I mentioned earlier, Reiki does not work based on a belief system. If you believe in Reiki or not, it will work if it is done right. Reiki isn't subject to religion at all. I can't force you to accept Reiki, but I can show you different ways in which Reiki is in line with Christianity.

- **Jesus was a healer**. This is acknowledged by every Christian that I know. There are a large number of occurrences in the Bible of Jesus healing people in body, mind, and soul.
- **Jesus said that all who gained from him would do the things he did - and that's just the beginning**. Jesus himself mentioned that those who believed in him would do even greater things than he did - and he happened to heal people, so of course you can, too!
- **Jesus instructed others to heal.** Jesus Christ wasn't some selfish superhero who kept his secrets to himself. He showed the majority of his devotees how to heal others and themselves, and frequently he would support their endeavors and correct them so they could go forth and heal others properly.

- **Jesus was caring**. Jesus showed love and sympathy, most importantly. He asked that we as a whole love and help our "neighbors," which He said is anybody and everybody. It appears he wanted everyone to get healing and love. He healed his believers just as the individuals who were of different societies and religions. Healing is not for a particular religion.
- **The early Christians appeared to understand that the art of healing was open to all**. The pieces of the new information that occurred after the passing of Jesus have numerous occasions of healing miracles done by Christ's disciples. Paul, specifically, visited healers and showed different devotees how to heal as well.

The main point of following the teachings of Christ is to gain some kind of knowledge and live by them. Healing is doing just that. Reiki healing is directly from God. This energy is from the Kingdom of Heaven, which is within you! *Why wouldn't you want to express it?* You see, Jesus had taught his followers how to generate and direct this energy for good.

Reiki is energy from God. Most see this energy as the essence of a higher power. It is a very spiritual practice and has helped a lot of Christians draw closer to God.

Chapter Two

REIKI SYMBOLS AND MEANINGS

Quick facts about Reiki, before we dive into the symbols:

- Reiki has a spiritual impact.
- Reiki is an extraordinary pain reliever.
- It works to heal the entire body
- It reduces pressure and tension.
- Fixes emotional problems.

Reiki can also be used for drawing in different things, including love, cash and success, so it's no big surprise many people are getting pulled in by Reiki now.

Reiki deals with healing without anyone else

Figuring out how to make positive changes in your life is a job you need to do on your own, and this can be done on a spiritual and mental level. Here is a basic example:

Sometimes it's like you don't just have enough money or love or friendship or happiness in your life. This could mean that possibly one of your chakras is blocked or there is something going on with you at a spiritual level. The next questions should be, "*What's going on here, and what can I do to fix this?*"

Usually, blockages are those negative feelings, those awful recollections, those bad energies. These are stresses, concerns, diversions and distractions. And these things block your chakra and affect the energies of your aura.

And if you want to, say, have money or progress or love, Reiki can be used to heal or unblock your chakras. What's more, you don't need anyone as you can do it by yourself, for yourself. Once these blockages start to vanish, you will start noticing progress in various aspects of your life. It's almost magical. You start feeling so much energy, joy and progress in your life.

The truth is, these beautiful feelings have always been inside and around you, but because you were blocked, you couldn't see or feel them. But that's okay. Everyone experiences a blockage every once in a while.

How to Use Reiki For Cash

In the event you wish to draw in cash and wealth, you should heal yourself first and attempt to take out all the negative trash with respect to cash. This will make you more confident and grounded so you can pull in affection, satisfaction, and long lasting friendship. You'll also find yourself receiving more cash inflow than you're used to. That sounds like a good deal, right?

The Symbols

Reiki healing is captivating to everyone, whether you practice it consistently or have had a Reiki session even once, or you literally just heard of it. The most fascinating aspects of Reiki, however, are the symbols. Reiki symbols help advance the healing process by gathering and centering the healing energy needed.

Reiki symbols basically tell the Reiki energy what to do and where to go. They also prepare the mind and body to receive the energy. During a healing session, the expert may either imagine the symbol, say their names out loud, or even draw them.

The Reiki symbols direct and center the energy frequency. I say frequency because each part of your body or level of your aura has a distinct frequency. So when you use the symbols, you tune the Reiki to the frequency of the area it needs to go. Let's look at some symbols:

Cho-Ku-Rei

This symbol represents the union between man and God. It increases the intensity or force of the Reiki energy. To get energy using this symbol, you should draw it on yourself or the person you're giving Reiki to and whisper the words Cho-Ku-Rei thrice and let the Reiki do its thing.

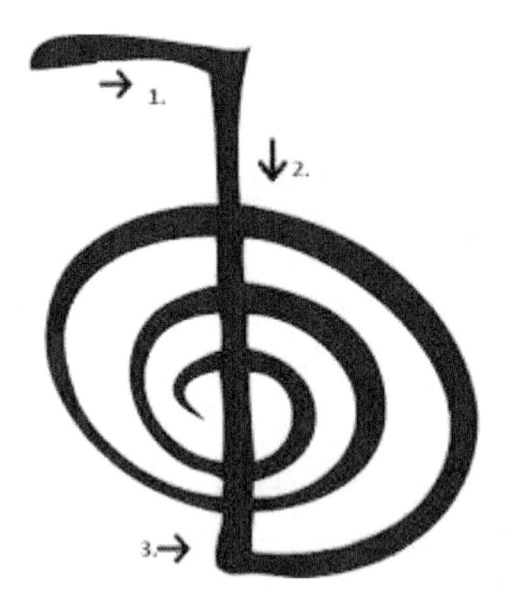

This symbol can also be used to clear out negative energy during your Reiki session. *Want to know a secret?* You can draw this symbol anywhere in your home to flush out bad vibes and attract positivity and light. You can also draw the symbol on business card or say the name right before an important business meeting to boost your chances of success.

Sei-Hei-Ki

This symbol is the way to the universe, people! It is usually used to heal the heart and quiet the brain. If you ever want to clear your head after a long day or a stressful problem, this is the symbol for you!

Hoping to retain new information, pass a test, or improve your memory as a whole? Sei-hei-ki can help with that. This symbol also helps in initiating a kind of Reiki called Kundalini Reiki which I will discuss soon.

Sei-Hei-Ki can surprisingly help with addiction and

past injuries, so it's your lucky day if you're a crack or sex addict. Sei-Hei-Ki is here for you. All you need to do is draw the symbol on the page of a book if you're going for memory improvement. You could also draw it on yourself during meditation or just imagine it in your head.

If you're trying to trash a negative behavior like excessive drinking or smoking, try picturing Sei-Hei-Ki in your mind. This helps quiet that mental battle going on in your head and over time, you'll find yourself less addicted to whatever it is you were addicted to in the first place.

Hon-Sha-Ze-Sho-Nen

This symbol is for separation. It is also the symbol of peace. This symbol is not like the rest. It does not affect the physical body per se, but it can influence it.

Hon

Sha

Ze

Sho

Nen

It is usually used to prepare for future healing and strengthen previous ones.

Tam A-Ra-Sha

This symbol is also called the unblocking symbol of Reiki. It is a very important symbol.

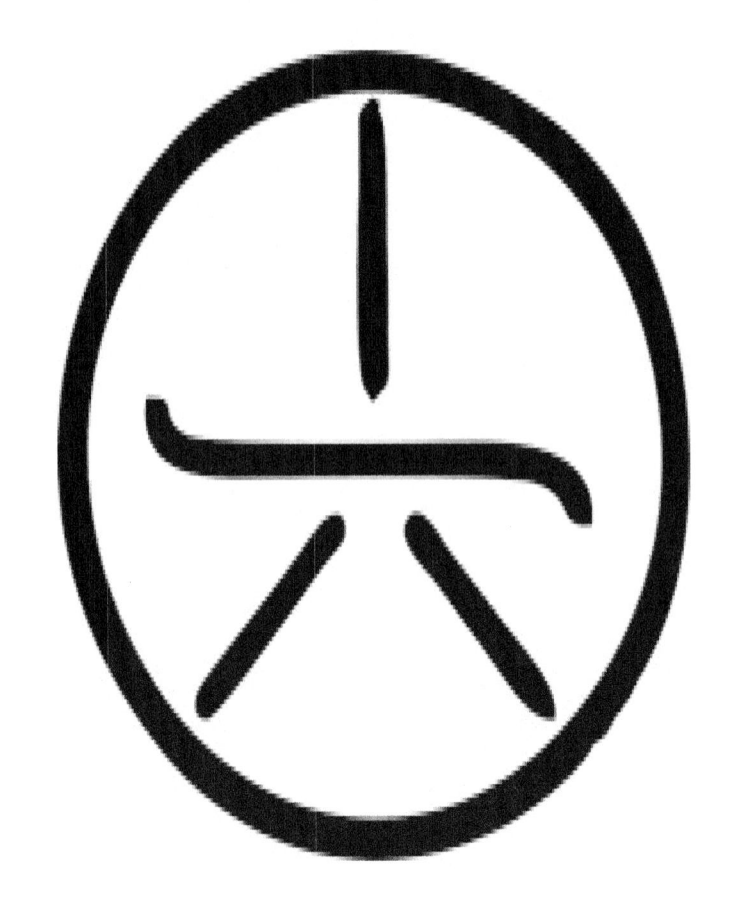

It helps to balance the energy while unblocking the chakra centers so the energy can flow freely.

Dai-Ko-Myo

This is simply the symbol of the masters. It is considered special among the dominant Reiki symbols because it can only be used by masters. *Sucks doesn't it?*

Dai Ko Myo

This symbol can help heal your spirit. It manages your spirituality by restoring you to your natural state of harmony. To fully understand how to use it, you have to become a Reiki master.

How to Activate The Reiki Symbols

To activate the Reiki symbols, you can do the following:

- Draw the symbols on the center of the palm.
- Draw the symbol on the center of your forehead.
- Draw them with your fingers.
- Picture them in your mind.

- Call out the name of the symbol multiple times.

Where Would It Be A Good Idea for You to Use The Symbols

- Most importantly, draw the symbol on the palm of your hand, and also draw them on your patient's hand or palm, or on the area where it is needed.

- If you can't seem to recall the symbol or how to draw it, you could always just say the name of the Reiki symbol out loud.
- After some time and with training, you will see that the symbols become less important, as you start to work with your instincts.

The Most Effective Method of Combining Reiki Symbols Together

Reiki symbols don't need to be used separately like most people think. They can be combined and used together. One way to do this is to combine different symbols for distant Reiki treatment. You should hold the picture of the person you intend to heal while you imagine the symbols in your mind. You could also say the names of the symbols multiple times. After you've done that, call the name of the person you want to send Reiki to, while still holding their photo of course.

Another way to combine Reiki symbols is to send numerous symbols to a future occasion you're anxious about; an interview maybe, or a blind date, even a medical checkup. Say the names of the symbols you want to send and imagine them bringing you joy and good news on the day of that occasion in question.

Now we've established the boundless benefits of Reiki, sometimes you might not have access to a Reiki session and you might really need one right about now. Don't be scared. You can be a Reiki healer and recipient at the same time. It's perfectly okay to perform Reiki on yourself in the event you can't get to a session.

More on Reiki Symbols

What everybody wants to know is which chakra is related to cash. And they will memorize just those symbols because they think that's the way to wealth and success. *Maybe that's how the Jenners did it.*

Sorry to burst your bubble guys, but there actually are no symbols for cash. There are symbols that are related to love, achievement, and wealth, however, none of them will make cash magically appear in your purse. For that, you will just have to work hard and take risks. Reiki is just there to assist you, to reveal your potential so you can do things that will draw in cash.

Since we're on the subject, for people who are searching for quicker approaches to cash, Reiki isn't a lottery. The main way to make progress, love, and cash is simply through work. Self-healing may take some time, and the outcomes are not quick, just so you know. You should put in certain months, or even years when using Reiki, so you can get lasting results.

The path of Reiki will take you through a process of deep self-healing, so you should invest a lot of energy to heal the negative energies towards cash in your life. You might even find hidden talents and all on this journey. Reiki can also be used for love if used correctly. Note that Reiki is not a love spell and will not enchant your partner!

A portion of the things you might experience during this Reiki journey includes:

1. You will notice the positive energy streaming into your life.
2. You will take care of yourself more without thinking too much about the costs.
3. You will notice all-round joy and prosperity.
4. You just might find the love of your life.
5. You will definitely look like a million bucks with great skin and even a positive vibe.
6. You would be more open for genuine companionships than before.

Chapter Three

REIKI HAND POSITIONS

A typical Reiki treatment has to do with the expert putting his or her hands on your body so the Reiki energy flows from their body into yours. There are no complicated rituals at all, just the straightforward transfer of energy between two people for the purpose of healing.

Like I said earlier, Reiki energy goes where it should and does what it should. A healer is just a channel; they have no power over the energy. so the best thing for the healer to do is nothing but stay out the way so Reiki can work.

When explaining Reiki to others, the hand positions should be the second thing you talk about, right after defining what Reiki is. Using the hand positions can be very helpful even though it is not always necessary as you advance in Reiki. The hand positions do the following:

- Cause us to become pathways for sending Reiki to various parts of the body.
- It helps create patience, since using all the hand positions should take about 40 minutes to an hour for a single treatment.

- It helps beginners to practice and control Reiki effectively when working with it, especially when healing yourself.

Most importantly, using hand positions enables us to play out a complete and whole-body Reiki treatment immediately, before we even start to expose ourselves to the whole "instinct" thing. You don't need to stress where to put your hands and send Reiki – simply take a look at your manual, booklet, or the photographs printed from the Web, and you got it!

I really recommend hand positions when you're a Reiki amateur. Using the positions you know about is really helpful regardless of whether you got them from your instructor, or a Reiki book, or here. What's more, don't stress, because Reiki will stream smoothly and with extraordinary advantages.

Yet, as time goes by as you work on yourself and practice various methods to facilitate personal growth, and as you regularly work with Reiki, you may see that your instincts ends up more grounded and focused. Instinct is that inward voice of direction we mostly call a "knowing" in your heart. Every living organism has a solid instinct, but most people do not know this and their minds are usually packed with unnecessary emotions and thoughts that can block this knowing.

In this way, individuals can't discern their instincts. With time, you will quiet down your mind as you fix your mental problems. For example, through Reiki, and spiritual growth practices such as yoga or meditation, your instincts kick in – on the grounds that they've always been there, and now you can decipher them accurately.

When your instincts starts to kick in, you automatically know where to put your hands, and that usually means *bye bye Reiki manual*. Try not to stress if you don't master the instinct thing for a couple of years (or much more) since you began working with Reiki. Take as much time as you need because each person develops at a different pace.

The Expert's Comfort

The healer's comfort is very important while preparing for Reiki. A full treatment can, without any interruption, keep going for an hour. If the patient is lying on the floor, how in the world can a human healer stay slouched over for that long? Isn't it better for the patient to be in a comfortable seat or a massage table for both their sakes?

So take that into consideration. Back rub tables are excellent for Reiki since they can be balanced, are comfortable, and allow the patient to loosen up totally. Some companies even make Reiki tables that have a move-around seat feature underneath. *Ha! How cool is that?*

Tips

Before you work on using your instincts, use the hand positions until you really get the hang of them. But most importantly, before you even attempt Reiki, you should keep the following in mind:

- **Keep in mind that when you send Reiki, you're a channel**. Clear your brain, relax and focus on your Hara, which lies in your stomach area. Remember, as a channel, Reiki moves through you. When you place your hands on a body - yours or another person's - let go. The body itself will feel the Reiki and draw it through your hands, and it will only take what it needs, so you don't need to worry. You are a channel, don't forget that.

- **Usually, I advise beginners to hold a hand positions for as long as 4 minutes before switching to another one.** Obviously, you don't need to touch the body, but if the patient specifically requests physical contact, by all means! You can just drift your hands an inch or so over the body. Don't worry, Reiki will still flow. You're a channel, not a blocked toilet pipe.

- **When you channel Reiki, your hands can be put on two separate pieces of the body, but your fingers should stick together**. But when you need to change hand positions, you can do that at any time, just keep your fingers close to each other and move your hands all at once.

- **Reiki will flow whether you're distracted or not**. It is okay to talk during Reiki or even get diverted. In fact, it is quite helpful. For instance, Reiki won't stop flowing out of your palms if you're talking to the patient or you're absent minded. If your patient wants to talk during treatment, by all means! Engage them. I mean, Reiki flows better when you're quiet and concentrated, but it will still flow even when you're not, so try not to look like an old potato. You might end up making your patient uncomfortable or even scared.

- **Try not to get tense**. Ensure both your muscles and mind are properly relaxed. Your body posture should be relaxed, as well.

Self-Healing

Sometimes, you might have a tight schedule, or a lot of kids, or you're just plain busy and you can't seem to find time for a Reiki appointment. There's always the option of healing yourself **by** yourself. It will take some time and a lot of practice, but it is doable, I assure you. The hand positions for self-healing are not quite the same as the ones for giving Reiki to someone else.

However, if you happen to make time for a Reiki appointment, you should ask about the difference between their hand positions and the ones you use on yourself. You never know what you might learn!

What Can Be Accomplished with Self-Healing?

Reiki self-healing can help various conditions like premenstrual syndrome (PMS), hypertension, allergies, joint pain, thyroid issues, and that's literally only the tip of the iceberg. Your problems won't magically disappear especially if you've been managing them for a while, but with steady Reiki practice, you should see obvious progress in a few weeks. I usually advise people to continue with Reiki even after their problems have been solved as some sort of maintenance practice. *You'll thank me later.*

Using All Hand Positions

If you're going to self-heal, try to use all the hand positions. You can make this easier by going from one body part to the other in this order:

- Crown of the head
- Face
- Throat
- Back of the head
- Upper chest
- Lower ribs
- Stomach catch
- Lower stomach area

Perfect Timing

A lot of people prefer to do their Reiki before they do anything else. You don't need to do this if it won't work for you. If you have to wake up early for work or school, you can try to squeeze Reiki into your tight schedule. It doesn't have to be done at a particular time of day. You just have to be consistent. And since you're self-healing, you make the rules.

When you start, you may need to ease into it. Don't rush. Try different things to figure out what works best for you. Remember, it's your journey. During the treatment, you may need to time yourself, especially if you have never done this before. You could use an alarm clock if you own one or your phone. This helps you use a particular hand position for a set time before switching to another one. It also helps you know when exactly to end a session.

Sometimes, you may not even complete the treatment for a lot of reasons, but that's okay, you're doing great. A little Reiki is better than no Reiki at all. Do what you can and continue the next day.

Switch It Up!

It is okay to change your routine every once in a while, but keep it as simple as possible because nobody likes a complicated routine. Reiki should not be used in place of medicines or herbs. It is only here to give your body the assistance it needs to recover. If you have asthma, Reiki is by no means a spiritual inhaler. Please see your doctor.

Before you start Reiki self-healing, you will need to focus on using the three Kanji hand positions:

- Position one - Try standing or sitting if you can. Put the tips of your index fingers together and intertwine the remaining fingers with each other. Close your eyes for a few seconds, maybe 20. Focus on your Reiki center which lies in your stomach area, around your navel.

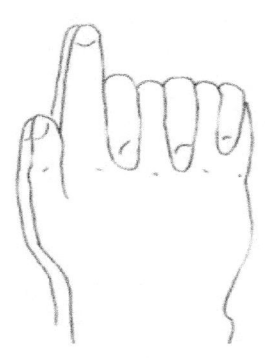

Position One

- Position two - This is almost the same as Position one except the middle fingers are touching this time and the remaining fingers are intertwined. Hold this for 25 minutes while picturing your Reiki center being filled with bright light.

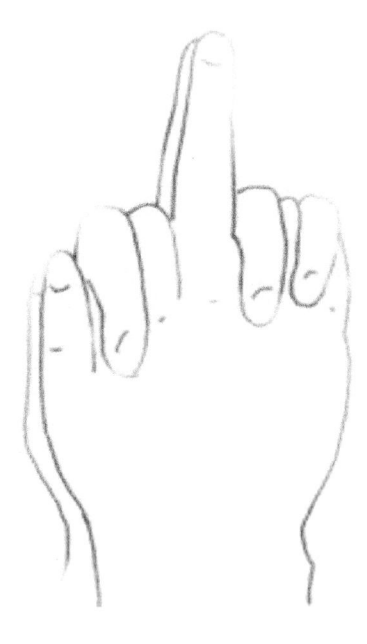

Position Two

- Position three - This position is different from the rest. Here, the fingers are laced together. Keep this position for 25 seconds while you allow energy to flow through your body.

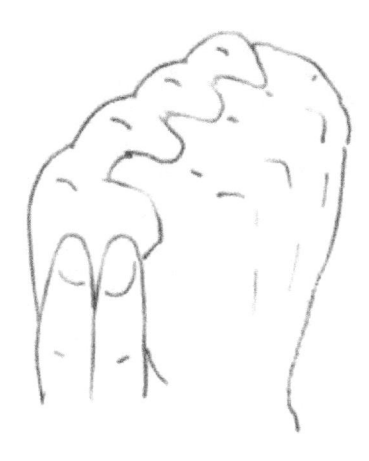

Position Three

After the three Kanji positions, feel free to lie down or sit in a comfortable position. Put a pillow underneath your knees if you wish. Cover yourself if you start to feel cold.

Now, turn your focus internally, and start to connect with your body. Begin with your head and sweep entirely through your body, down to your tippy toes. How do you feel in each part of your body?

- Is there any kind of pressure?
- Can you fix it?
- Do you feel any pain in certain parts of your body?
- Can you make it go away?

- Can you tell what is causing you to feel pain? Since you are focused and prepared for healing, you can start giving yourself Reiki.

    1. **Position one** - Put your hands over your face with your fingers at the highest point of your brow with your hands touching.
    2. **Position two (a)** - Place your hands over your head. Your fingertips must be touching.
    3. **Position two (b)** - Alternate position to Position two- Place your hands over your ears, massaging them slowly and softly.
    4. **Position three** - Place your hands on the back of your head, the base of your palms at the base of the skull.
    5. **Position four** - Place your left hand over your heart and your right hand over your throat
    6. **Position five** - Cross your arms at your elbows and place two hands over your shoulders near your neck.
    7. **Position six** - Place both of your hands with fingers touching over your upper stomach area, simply cup your ribs.
    8. **Position seven** - Place your hands over your belly with fingers touching at your navel.

9. **Position eight** - Place your hands over your lower belly with your fingertips over your pubic bone.
10. **Position nine** - Place your hands over your lower back. Your fingertips must be touching.
11. **Position ten** - Place your hands over your lower back with your fingertips over your lower spine.
12. **Position eleven** - Hold your left foot with both your hands.
13. **Position twelve** - Hold your right foot with both your hands.
14. **Position thirteen** - Hold your left foot with your left hand and right foot with right hand.
15. **Position thirteen(b) -** Hold your right foot with left hand and left foot with right hand.

Reiki self-healing is very basic and you should feel comfortable while holding these positions. If you can't hold your feet for instance, you can send long distance Reiki. You don't need to have direct contact with your body. Simply point your palms towards your feet and close your eyes while imagining you are holding them.

Reiki for Treatment

Before you throw on a doctor's hat and start treating others, there are some important things to know. Think of them as rules of the trade.

- Never give a Reiki treatment to anyone who has a pacemaker. A pacemaker is a device put in the chest to help a person whose heart can't beat very well. This device releases electric signals to the heart and Reiki can interrupt these signals, which can cause even worse problems than an irregular heartbeat. It's going to be like giving roasted turkey to a 10 year old with braces.
- Never give a Reiki treatment to anyone who is suffering from diabetes. Treatment for diabetes is usually an insulin injection every day. Reiki energy can affect the levels of insulin in the body. Reiki is safer when the person can produce insulin just fine on their own and people with diabetes cannot, that is why they

need insulin injections. You don't want to mess with their insulin reserve.
- It is advised to talk to your patient before you perform any kind of Reiki on them. Let them know exactly what you are going to do, how it will affect them, and what they should expect in general. Make them understand that it is completely normal and they have nothing to fear. Working with a completely relaxed patient is better than a totally paranoid one, so do what you can to help them relax.

During a Reiki healing session, your patient may experience:.

- Cold
- Heat
- Memory flashbacks
- They might even doze off
- Immediate improvements
- Rumbling stomach
- Feeling like they have needles all over their body.
- Phantom Hands
- Irritation

- Pain

Most of the time, your patient will feel cold wherever you place your hands while you, the healer, will feel a lot of heat at the same spot or the other way around. If, however, your patient doesn't feel anything after expecting to feel so much, let them know it's okay, because Reiki affects people in different ways.

Always remember, the patient is drawing Reiki through you. They are healing themselves, and you are just a channel. You don't need to have a PhD in human anatomy or physiology before you treat a person or yourself with Reiki. Just connect with your patient through your hands and let Reiki flow. Don't forget to use your instincts if you can.

Focus on your patient, pay attention to their body language. Jerking movement or moans is a great sign that they feel what you are doing. The typical time for a full body treatment is between 50 minutes to 90 minutes. When you finish, wash your hands and drink some water. You deserve it.

Begin Treatment

Be certain your patient is lying straight on the

treatment table with their arms somewhere near their sides. Their legs should also be straight against the table and should not be crossed because this might confuse Reiki. Softly put your hands on your patient's body, and let them sit there for three to six minutes, or till whenever your instincts tell you.

Your fingers should be touching always. Keep your hands like you're trying to hold imaginary water but facing your patient's body. This keeps a solid connection between you and your patient. Any tiny space between your fingers will let the Reiki escape, same as water.

We do not let things slip through our fingers!

Err... When you get to a patient's **bosoms** or **privates**, just let your hand hover over them. **Do. Not. Touch.**

Now that you have a pretty good picture of things, we can take a closer look at the hand positions for treating patients.

- **Position 1**

    Cup your hands and delicately rest them over your patient's eyes, cheekbones and brow (third eye chakra). This position is for stress, eye issues, asthma, allergies, fever, nerve damage, brain problems, and sinusitis.

- **Position 2**

    Place your hand over your patient's head with your palms covering the crown chakra. This position is for headaches, eye issues, migraines, stress, multiple sclerosis, bladder problems, stomach-related issues, and emotional issues.

- **Position 3**

    Put your hands on both sides of your patient's head with your fingers covering their temples. This position is for ear problems, colds, flu and left brain problems.

- **Position 4**

    Put your hands on the back of your patient's head covering the entire area. This position is for migraines, eye issues, stress, fever, sinusitis, stomach related issues, fears, depression and stroke.

- **Position 5**

    Place your hands along the patient's jawbone

covering their throat chakra. This position helps with breathing, bronchitis, self-expression, voice and communication issues, flu, and the common cold.

- **Position 6**

   Place your hands along the patient's shoulders. This position is for the elbows, arms, cold hands, tight shoulder muscles, stress, poor movement or poor blood supply to the arms and hands.

- **Positions 7**

   Put your hands over the T covering the neckline bone and heart chakra.

- **Positions 8-9**

   From Position 7, move your hands down the front of the body and over it covering the solar plexus and sacral chakras.

- **Position 10**

   Make a V with your hands and use it to cover the root chakra

- **Positions 11-12**

   At last, place your hands over your patient's

knees and feet. It works on the body organs.

Now that you have finished the hand positions for the front of the body, gently tell your patient to turn over so you can start to take a shot at the hand positions for the back of the body. If your patient has dozed off, softly wake them up.

- **Position 13**

    Start by setting your hands over your patient's shoulders

- **Positions 14,15,16**

    Now, you should move your hands down their back. This position is for the solar plexus chakra, the sacral chakra and the heart chakra.

- **Position 17**

    Use your hands to make a T to cover the root chakra.

- **Positions 18 and 19**

    Finally, the last positions. Place your hands on the back of your patient's feet and knees. These positions are for joint aches, back pain and spinal issues, anger issues, stress, feelings, leg aches, varicose veins and poor mobility. Or you could just treat every single organ through the reflexology points in your patient's feet.

Side note: Reflexology is a kind of alternative medicine that involves applying pressure on specific points of your feet. It is believed that certain points of the feet are connected to certain organs in the body.

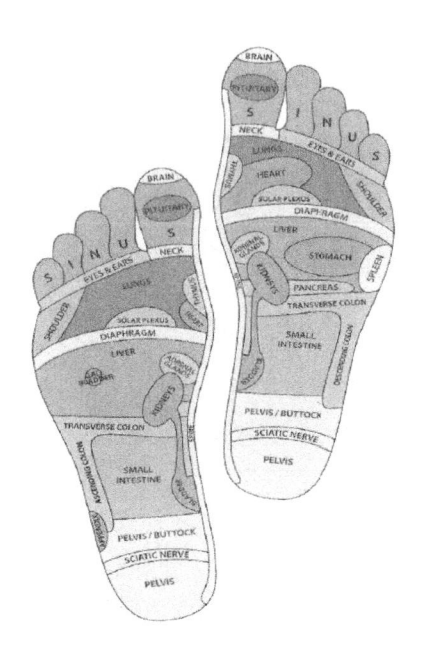

When every one of the positions have been properly executed, place your right hand at the base of your patient's spine and your left hand on their crown chakra.

This position balances the Reiki energy they just received. Brush through your patient's aura with your fingers by lightly hovering your palms over the body, stroking it from the crown of their head to the feet until your hand touches the floor in a single smooth movement. Do this a few more times than once, before you send them on their way to enjoy a Reiki filled life.

Chapter Four

CHAKRAS

"Chakra" is a Sanskrit word that literally translated to **'wheel'**. Chakras are like energy centers in your body. They are located at specific points of the body. They were named according to the roundish shape of the energy centers that exist on our spiritual bodies.

There are seven chakras known to man and they are found along the length of the spine. Each chakra has special characteristics that can be compared to the characteristics of the area of the body in which they are found starting from the root chakra at the base of the spine, to the crown chakra at the top of the head. These chakras are also related to specific colors believed to be the actual colors of the chakras if they could be seen with the naked eye.

Studying chakras is a very important aspect of Reiki because Reiki, as I said earlier, is lifeforce. It is energy. And these chakras are energy centers in the body. Reiki flows through the chakras to the rest of your body.

Imagine a lightbulb in a small room. The lightbulb needs electricity to work and wires are like tiny roads that electricity takes to get to where it is needed. When the wire transfers this electricity to the lightbulb, the lightbulb automatically comes on and brightens the small room. Now imagine the wire is the Reiki healer, the current is Reiki, the lightbulb is your chakra and the small room is your body. Understand?

These chakras have the ability to absorb, change and transfer energy. We literally wouldn't be able to exist without them because they provide the 'electricity' we need to survive. They are like powerhouses we can't see.

Each chakra in your body is connected to a particular area in the body and the organs surrounding it. And because the chakras are evenly spread, every organ in your body has a chakra it is connected to. There's always one in the area!

The sizes and activity of the chakras are different for everybody. They work at different paces and levels with regard to the individual and their current ability to transfer energy through your body.

The lower chakras usually deal with emotions, feelings of anger, love, passion. While the higher chakras deal with logic, intelligence, thoughts, and anything spiritual, really.

Your chakras depend on you to function, and if you don't take care of them, they won't do much for you until you do. A lot of things can affect your chakras negatively and positively. Meditation, yoga, certain precious stones, diet, and other lifestyle changes can alter the effectiveness of your chakras.

Chapter Five

THE ROOT CHAKRA

The Root Chakra is also called the Miladhara. This the very first chakra, and it is located at the base of the spine. Reach behind you and try to touch your butt. Soft, right? Good, take your hand higher. Still soft? Higher then. You should feel a bony structure right on your waist. **That** is the base of your spine and the location of your root chakra.

Okay you can stop squeezing your squishy butt now, you weirdo.

When everything is great with this chakra, that means it is not blocked by any negative energy or junk you might be holding onto in your mind from the past. And this means you'll feel safe, secure, and at peace in your environment. You'll feel this burst of energy surging through you all the time. *Almost like you could take on even Superman and knock him out so hard he wakes up in Krypton.*

Having a balanced or clear root chakra is very important. A balanced or clear root chakra is a chakra that is not blocked at all. Think of your root chakra as a kitchen drain. Usually, water should flow smoothly through the drain. But when your baby sister decides to be a sous chef and ends up stuffing more vegetables in the drain than in the salad bowl, the water doesn't go through.

The kitchen drain wasn't built for vegetables, so it gets blocked, and water can't pass through anymore. What do we do? We call a plumber or unblock the drain ourselves, right? This is exactly how the root chakra and pretty much every chakra works. Except besides draining out the bad energy, it also recharges your body, mind, and spirit with good, clear energy.

Physical Location: The base of your spine (where your tailbone is found).

Component: Earth.

Color: Red.

Signs of a Blocked Root Chakra: If your root chakra is blocked you may feel lost, terrified or on edge. This feeling of uneasiness can take over your mind, making your paranoia go from zero to a hundred. You start to feel unsure about everything; that interview, that romantic date, that college course... You won't be able to focus on anything at all and that equals stress, which equals eye bags, which equals more concealer. A blocked root chakra can also cause you pain in your lower body. *Not cool at all.*

What Is The Root Chakra Responsible For?

Experts on the subject were more than happy to let us know that a blocked root chakra is the reason a lot of us are crazy, paranoid creatures. The root chakra deals with safety and survival. The state of your root chakra determines if you'll move forward in life or if you should get a pillow and get comfortable where you're at. Understanding this chakra will help you spot blockages on time and do what is necessary to fix it. By starting with the root chakra, I am laying the foundation for the other six chakras.

Muladhara which is another name for the root chakra - as I've already mentioned - literally means **root base**. This is because it is located at the base of your spine and deals with anything that concerns your security.

For instance, it affects and is affected by the following:

- How safe you feel.
- Your ability for survival.
- The feeling of security.
- Your basic needs (for example water, and rest).
- How often you feel the need to change and develop.

To know if your chakra is blocked, you'll feel anything but a sense of safety. If your root chakra is fine, you will feel relaxed, steady, and just alright really!

The tricky thing about the root chakra is it can just wind up blocked on a good day if your safety feels threatened even a tiny bit.

How to know if your root chakra is blocked

A wonky root chakra can really throw your entire system for a loop, leaving you feeling awkward and unsettled. The most common symptoms and indications of a blocked Root Chakra are:

- Your paranoia goes through the roof.
- Your hands and feet may start to feel cold.
- You begin to have major trust issues.
- You may find yourself hyperventilating or having some other anxiety problem.
- You may feel uneasy in your stomach
- You. Just. Can't. Focus.
- You and food get into a toxic relationship.
- You start doubting yourself and everything around you
- You always wonder what people think about you.
- Your back and leg start to hurt.
- You fall into a pit of depression.

Most times, you may not know what blocked your root chakra in the first place, but it's good to remember anything that makes you full of doubt and trust issues is a root chakra blocker. For example, a bad breakup, financial issues, losing a job, bad criticism, serial killers, Prince Joffrey, and so on.

I'm here to help you realize how to recognize these triggers and know exactly what to do to keep your root chakra in check.

How to unblock your root chakra

1.   Root Chakra Stones And Jewelry

Fixing up your root chakra is not as complicated as that YouTube video you watched. You can unblock your root chakra with certain precious stones by either holding them in your palm or wearing them as jewelry. The root chakra has four major precious stones. They are :

- **Red Jasper.** The root chakra's color is red so you shouldn't be so surprised when a root chakra gemstone happens to share the same color. This stone deals with emotional balance, so it's a perfect stone to have if your feelings happen to be all over the place.

- **Red Carnelian.** A light red that looks a bit orangey, red carnelian deals with letting go, energy, and bravery. It is the stone for you if you find yourself being indecisive and can't seem to find a way out of your comfort zone.

- **Obsidian.** A dark gemstone, obsidian is said to shield you from damage. You may draw some solace from wearing it as you work to move to a position of more prominent security in your life.

- **Bloodstone.** The stone itself is green. The name **bloodstone** is due to its red spots. This semi-valuable stone has to do with pushing endless negative energy and building confidence, so if you find yourself being sucker-slapped in the face by life, this is the ideal stone for you.

2. Root Chakra, Yoga and Meditation.

Meditation and yoga fix almost everything. Having back pain? Meditation and yoga. Sleeping problems? Meditation and yoga. Can't find the tissue? Meditation and yoga!

The root chakra meditation technique can really help ease up your blocked chakra. Meditation for this chakra is actually very similar to normal meditation techniques, except that when meditating for the root chakra, you have to concentrate only **on** the root chakra.

Try this straightforward and successful root chakra meditation technique:

- Sit with your shoulders back and your spine straight. Try to loosen up a bit. Let your muscles be at complete rest. Now, close your eyes and inhale deeply. Breathe in through your nose, pulling the breath as far down into your body as you can and then breathe through your mouth.
- Focus completely on your root chakra, nowhere else. Keep your concentration on the area directly beneath your tailbone. Take note of how you feel at this point.
- We all know the root chakra's color is red, so you'll need to imagine a ball of red light growing at the base of your spine. Watch this red light grow even brighter, making the area beneath your tailbone feel relaxed and a bit warm. Stay like this for 4-6 minutes.
- When you're prepared, gradually open your eyes. Sit still for a couple of minutes before going about your daily routine.

3. **Changing your diet**

Other ways to improve your root chakra activities include rolling out little improvements to your eating regimen. *I'm just saying, you are what you eat.*

Experts on the subject discovered how much influence our diet has on our chakras. Besides, most of the foods for a healthy root chakra will also lead to a healthy you in general, so what do you have to lose? Apart from all that butter and cellulite, of course.

In any case, there are specific foods that are directly linked to the root chakra. Anything natural is a brilliant choice because the root chakra is usually opened with anything associated with roots. Let's take a look:

- **Protein-rich food.** Protein is a bodybuilder, and will help ground you and provide physical as well as the spiritual energy. Examples are tofu, green peas, spinach, beans and almonds.
- **Any red fruits.** Because the root chakra is red, red fruits go a long way in unblocking that chakra. *I know it looks absolutely ridiculous but trust me.* Besides, red foods pump you full of vitamin C as a little something extra for your immune system. Check out tomatoes, red cherries, strawberries, red peppers and so on.
- **Root vegetables** like beets, garlic, and potatoes are on the table as well, somewhat on

account of the fact that they develop **in the ground**. Their ability to unblock your root chakra is because these veggies have energy from the ground in them, which is perfect for your root chakra.

4. **Use of Root Chakra Affirmations**

Words are more powerful than we give them credit for. What we say to and about ourselves can affect us in a powerful way. This can be negative or positive. If you look at yourself in the mirror every day and tell yourself you will never be beautiful, you will never be beautiful - not because you are not, but because everyone one will see you the way you see yourself.

That being said, there are certain affirmations for unblocking or healing the root chakra. And just like all affirmations, you can say them every day, anytime and anywhere, or whenever you feel a root chakra block coming on. You can try any or all of the following:

1. I am secure and protected wherever I go.
2. I am ready to be directed and guided by the universe.

3. Today, I am relaxed, steady, and secure.
4. I feel happy and safe in my home.
5. I do not want for anything. I am content.
6. I feel connected to the earth and protected by the universe
7. I get whatever I want because the universe is on my side.
8. I feel myself relaxing as my root chakra is opening.
9. I am happy, I am healthy, and I am loved.
10. The universe will always be here for me.

Just like Reiki symbols, these root chakra fixers can be combined and used together. You could get into a Yoga position while holding one of the chakra stones or saying one of the chakra affirmations. Some people prefer to record their affirmations and play them like music while they meditate. This puts a certain light in them as they go about their daily lives. That happy-go-lucky coworker might have just unlocked her root chakra!

Chapter Six

THE SACRAL CHAKRA

The Sacral Chakra is the second chakra. It's also called **Svadhishthana,** which is Sanskrit, and it literally translates as "one's own dwelling." It is found in the stomach area, underneath the navel. and is strictly involved with your imaginative energy.

When people think imagination, they think beauty and creativity. But there is more to the imagination than aesthetics, and certainly more to your sacral chakra than all that. There is also your sexuality and your ability to change or adapt to your environment.

Your Sacral chakra can end up getting blocked if you're somehow worried about your sexuality or your new environment. It could also be affected by how satisfied you are in your relationship.

Or by negative criticism on something you've worked so hard for. *That's never pretty.*

Physical Location: The stomach area. Underneath the navel.

Component: Water

Color: Orange.

Signs of a Blocked Sacral Chakra: When there's

an issue with the Sacral Chakra, you're probably going to feel exhausted, drowsy and almost depressed. You will have a low sex drive and you will be absolutely terrified of change. On the physical side, you might have urinary problems and certain allergies. You may also have addictions - and not the drinking kind. The eating kind, or excessive shopping, or even an addiction to gambling.

What Is The Sacral Chakra Responsible For?

A lot of things can affect or be affected by the Sacral Chakra. I'll list a few.

- How motivated you feel.
- Your ability to have fun with other people.
- How you feel about the things you create
- How satisfied you are in your relationships

- Your creativity.
- How much joy you feel in general
- Your interest in sexual activities

Now we know what can affect or be affected by your sacral chakra. At whatever point your sacral chakra is open, you'll feel full of life, ready for change and filled with inspiration. Also, when this chakra is balanced and unblocked, you'll feel more confident about making certain changes in your life that you never knew you could make.

On the other hand, your sacral chakra can be pushed out of alignment by anything exhausting, or suffocating. For example, if someone makes rude remarks about your art project or sexuality, and you start to doubt yourself and your capabilities, then this feeling of doubt can block your sacral chakra.

Side effects of a Blocked Sacral Chakra

Like any chakra, the sacral chakra has the ability to make you feel completely out of it. The most common sacral chakra issues and side effects are listed below:

- Overwhelming exhaustion.
- Bladder uneasiness.

- Low energy.
- Feeling mostly annoyed.
- Zero determination.
- Absence of imaginative motivation
- Allergies
- Fear of change.
- Blame about the past.
- Low self-esteem
- Low sex drive
- Addictive practices, like excessive drinking, shopping, unhealthy eating habits, gambling, and so on.

It is okay to feel all these things and not be able to pinpoint exactly what caused your chakra to become blocked. However, you should remember that anything to do with change, sexuality and creativity can push your Sacral chakra out of position. Some examples include:

- Sexual problems in a relationship
- Loss of a job
- Dismissal of your creative content (anything from a book to a business idea)
- Recurrent medical issues

How to unblock your Sacral chakra

You'll be doing yourself and the people around you a favour when you finally figure out how to unblock most or all of your chakras. Unblocking even one of your chakras will go a long way in ensuring your physical, spiritual, emotional and mental survival. With the Sacral Chakra unblocked, you'll be better than anyone at foresight, creativity and control over your sexuality. You'll be filled to the brim with confidence, feel more connected emotionally to others, you will be able to let go of old blame and accept positive changes in your life. You may also see yourself feeling genuine happiness and expressing your feelings more appropriately.

1. **Sacral Chakra Stones And Jewelry**

There are certain stones that have strong links to each of your chakras. Every one of them can be carried in your purse, or just held onto, or kept in your home. Here are the major sacral chakra stones worth finding:

Orange calcite: The sacral chakra's color is orange so obviously; a large number of sacral healing stones are orange too. Orange calcite, also called the **mind**

stone, is believed to improve the imagination. It can also help you move past emotional blockages and enter into a balance between your body and your mind. This stone is a link between the physical and the spiritual and is the stone usually recommended for people with phobias.

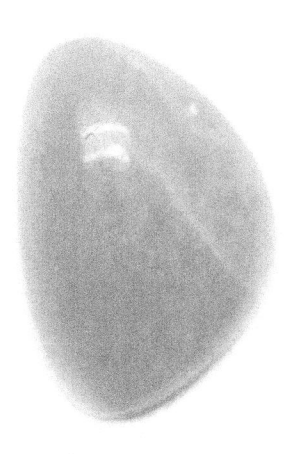

Moonstone: The moonstone, also known as the **traveller's stone** because of the protection it provides especially at night, comes in a lot of colors. However, I strongly recommend the peach colored moonstone because of the way it affects the brain. It reduces stress and fills you with energy. However, you might need to decide on the peach moonstone because of its incredible ability to lessen stress and convey a sort of soothing, calming energy. It particularly supports emotional and sensitive people.

Carnelian: This semi-valuable gemstone has a rosy dark colored tone, but it can come in different shades. It is also called **the Singer's stone**. It is the stone to have if you have a performance to prepare for, whether on stage or in between the sheets. Nudge nudge, wink wink.

Citrine: Citrine stones are a brilliant yellow color and they're sometimes called the "stones of the brain." It is the stone for confidence as it carries the light of the sun. Citrine is also used for fixing Interpersonal relationships, as it improves communication.

2. Sacral Chakra Meditation And Yoga Techniques

Sacral chakra meditation is quite different from basic meditation techniques, because it involves direct focus on your navel region. If you practice meditation or yoga or even both regularly, you can add these techniques to the mix. Since you're already meditating, why not show some love to your Sacral chakra while you're at it? Try this as soon as you get the chance. I highly recommend it!

1. Sit in a comfortable calm spot where you won't be irritated. Keep your spine straight, and your legs and arms loose.
2. Take ten moderate, full breaths.
3. Picture a turning orange ball of light in the area of your sacral chakra.
4. Since the sacral chakra's element is water, imagine the orange light rolling out in smooth waves like the ocean. Allow yourself to be covered by this wave of orange light. You might start to feel your entire body heating up now.
5. Do this for whatever length of time that you like (ideally six minutes). Now open your eyes when you feel prepared.

Yoga can be combined with your chakra work. Any yoga practice will help with your chakras, yet there are particular exercises for the sacral chakra.

When you can, try to do **Dvipada Pitham**, which includes lying on your back and lifting your hips while you lift your arms up and over your head. Let your shoulders carry your body weight all through this exercise. This is probably the best sacral chakra workout you might find!

Chakra Diet Suggestions

The majority of the chakras react to your eating regimen, so you can possibly unblock the sacral chakra just by making little changes to what you eat. Healthy eating habits are useful for keeping up open chakras, but right now we're going to take a look at foods that have direct links to your sacral chakra.

Oranges: Obviously! Orange is the color that speaks to your sacral chakra, so it shouldn't be very surprising that oranges help with sacral chakra healing. Other orange fruits can also help. Fruits like pawpaws, mangoes and peaches.

Seeds: I personally recommend eating a lot of seeds if you're in the business of unblocking your sacral chakra. Some seeds are sunflower seeds, poppy seeds, pumpkin seeds and hemp seeds.

Coconuts: Coconuts are very healthy in general, seeing as they contain healthy fats that help keep your heart happy. They also help maintain your energy levels and increase your ability to be creative. *Looking for inspiration on a project? Try munching on some coconuts!*

Tea and smoothies: Fluids are very good for our physical health as we all know. Certain teas and vegetables smoothies have been tested and trusted to fix up your sacral chakra in no time.

4. **Sacral Chakra Affirmations To Use**

As you most definitely know, using your words to change your situation and how you feel about yourself is one of ways to balance your sacral chakra. All you have to do is say anything positive about issues concerning your sacral chakra and mean it. It won't work unless you mean it. I made a list of various affirmations you could use but if what you need isn't on my list, feel free to create your own! It's really not rocket science. Just think of a terrible situation in your life, turn the story around and speak your truth. Let's see some examples.

- I have a right to joy and contentment
- It is okay to express my sexual self for no particular reason, in acceptable ways
- I am sure that I am enough
- I will always be full of joy, laughter, and kindness
- I am surrounded by people who motivate me

- I am not afraid of change. I've got this!
- I am full of motivation and bursting with creativity
- My body is beautiful and I am comfortable inside it
- I am prepared for constructive change and self-awareness
- I am a strong, imaginative person, and I adore what I create

Chapter Seven

THE SOLAR PLEXUS CHAKRA

The Solar Plexus Chakra is the third chakra and it is located around the stomach region, at the highest point of your mid-region. It's also called **Manipura**, which is Sanskrit. It literally means "shining jewel." This chakra is the center for identity, personality, self-sufficiency, confidence and assurance. Sometimes it is called the **individual power** chakra.

When all is right with your **manipura**, you will have a clear path in front of you. You will be able to understand what you need to do to move forward. You will feel freer than you've ever felt and you will be able to achieve anything you set your mind to do. *Now how's that for a life boost?*

However, like all things, this can be negatively affected by certain things like lingering emotions from bad experiences, disappointments, undesirable gatherings, and so on

Physical Location: Around the stomach area at the highest point of your mid-region.

Component: Fire

Color: Yellow.

Signs of Blocked Solar Plexus Chakra: If there's

a blockage around the solar plexus chakra, your certainty might be extremely unstable. If there is even just a little blockage, there may just be uncertainty in one particular area of your life. A bigger blockage can cause major confidence issues. You might start drowning in self-doubt, thinking you're not good enough or capable enough to learn from your mistakes. You start forgetting little things and making unnecessary mistakes. Physically, your tummy might hurt. A lot.

What Is The Solar Plexus Chakra Responsible For?

Any of the following can affect the solar plexus chakra, or can be affected by it:

- How you react to information from other

individuals

- Wondering whether you can take lessons from challenges
- Wondering whether you consider yourself to be "good enough"
- How you see yourself and your life's goal.
- Your ability for self-forgiveness.
- Your self-control.
- Your autonomy.

This means an open solar plexus chakra will guarantee you feel confident, sure of your own personality, and certain about what you have to do to succeed.

Then again, your solar plexus chakra can be shut or slightly put out of alignment by anything that undermines you, by abrupt changes throughout your life, or by troubles related with moving on from past mistakes. Strangely, chakra specialists have speculated that you can have an overactive solar plexus chakra, making you act crazy or really nervous. *So that's why I get hyper sometimes. Huh.*

Blocked Solar Plexus Chakra

Now that everyone understands the importance of the solar plexus chakra, we can now look at what occurs during a blockage. Here are the most basic solar plexus chakra issues and side effects that are connected to blockages:

- Having thoughts that you have to control everything and everybody around you.
- Uncertain blame about the past.
- Feeling defenseless.
- Stomach related issues.
- Trouble seeing the "big picture" throughout everyday life
- Absence of direction
- Low confidence
- Troubles with memory.
- Dreams that need direction and guidance.
- Queasiness
- Swelling in your stomach (bloating)

On the off chance you have a minor blockage, your reduced or absent confidence or desire may just be in one part of your life (communication, work or relationships), while a greater blockage will be connected to all around low confidence and can even have you feeling utterly useless.

When you have a blocked solar plexus chakra, you won't generally be able to pinpoint the origin of the issue. Anyhow, whenever you do end up with negative solar plexus side effects, take some time to find out if your confidence or sense of reason has been threatened lately.

For instance, maybe somebody has made fun of you when you confided in them about what you need to do with your life. Or possibly, you are going through something and are trying so hard to find the best way to move forward. Or you just had rotten tomatoes for dinner.

When you have a better handle on precisely how you can push balance your solar plexus chakra once again, you'll additionally turn out to be better at detecting the sorts of things that may block that chakra. With time, aligning and unblocking your solar plexus chakra will be a piece of cake.

While it is a smart thought to dedicate time to learning all the chakras as each one offers unique advantages, focusing on the solar plexus chakra is going to help you be a better decision maker, a person filled with positivity and confidence and a healthy individual in general.

Regardless of whether you need to discover a new relationship, get promoted or expand in some way, independence, confidence and charisma are fundamental. During this exercise, you will also experience spiritual and mental enlightenment, and as a little something extra, you'll have no more issues with your stomach. Since the solar plexus chakra has a great deal to do with life goals, clearing it up decreases procrastination.

So taking care of your solar plexus chakra can enable you make good use of opportunities as they come with regards to a better and brighter future.

We'll go now to take a look at four special ways you can unblock your solar plexus chakra.

- **Solar Plexus Chakra Stones And Jewelry**

As you likely know, all stones and gems have old uses and connections to chakras. All things considered; it is pretty obvious that there are stones particular to each chakra. You can use these stones in a tremendous amount of ways when opening chakras. You may wear solar plexus chakra necklaces or bracelets, or hold a stone in the palm of your hand when meditating, or basically carry one in your pocket to help keep your solar plexus in alignment throughout the day. Here are the stones most connected with solar plexus chakra:

- **Amber**: Your solar plexus chakra is yellow, not unlike amber stones. These stones are also called "**gold of the ocean.**" The amber stone is not a gem per se, but a product of nature. It is formed from old fossils through a process called polymerisation. Amber stones are orangey-yellow in color, and they are connected to both confidence and mental clarity. Use this stone in case you're attempting to settle on a choice.

- **Yellow tourmaline**: Yellow tourmaline is physically striking, and you'll frequently see it sold as a "detox" stone. It cleanses your solar plexus chakra and converts negative energy to positive energy.

- **Citrine**: Another yellow solar plexus gem, this pale stone is in some cases called the "achievement stone" or "the stone of the brain." It is the stone for confidence as it carries the light of the sun.

2. Solar Plexus Meditation And Yoga Techniques

Solar plexus chakra meditation techniques for beginners are anything but difficult to do, whether or not you have a fundamental knowledge on meditation and yoga. They always start with a few minutes of deep breathing, and after that once you're appropriately relaxed and focused, you can move onto a position that helps you get to the solar plexus chakra:

- Shut your eyes and direct your concentration toward your upper stomach area, where the solar plexus chakra is.
- Picture a round circle of shining yellow light in the center point of the upper stomach area, and gradually focus on making the energy bigger and brighter.
- While your eyes are still closed, envision the circle turning clockwise as it blossoms, and feel the region getting hotter. Please relax as you do this.
- Following 3-6 minutes, let the energy flow all through your body. Take a couple of full breaths again, and open your eyes.

You can also add yoga postures to your daily routine if you feel you need to adjust or unblock the solar plexus chakra. Specialists on chakra work normally support all types of yoga, however, specific positions help you better connect with your solar plexus chakra. Like the child's pose, which goes like this:

- Put a very soft cover or pad under your knees.
- Stoop down, sitting on your heels
-

- Move your knees so they are separated slightly.
- Lean down so your chest area sits between your thighs.
- Stretch out your hands on the floor, palms down in front of you, while you elongate your back gently. Hold the pose and breathe.

3. **Solar Plexus chakra and diet**

Increasing fiber intake, decreasing sugar and completely reducing the sheer amount of saturated fat in your eating routine are extraordinary for your chakras. However, there are certain chakra foods directly linked to the solar plexus and they can accelerate solar plexus chakra alignment:

- **Yellow peppers**: Since yellow is the color of the solar plexus chakra, you can't turn out badly when adding yellow peppers to your meals whenever you can.
- **Complex starches**: Given that the solar plexus chakra takes on a major job in the energy-giving department, it's advisable to go for nourishment that gives you a continued supply of energy rather than only a spike in sugar levels. Awesome examples are dark

colored rice, darker bread, and wholegrain grain.

- **Corn**: Another yellow food, corn can feed the solar plexus chakra and give your progress and confidence an additional lift. It is frequently the main solar plexus food mentioned in a beginner's manual for chakras.
- **Chamomile tea**: While not technically nourishment, chamomile tea has dependably been prescribed to help treat a solar plexus chakra blockage. It can also settle an irritated stomach and help you lose weight.

4. **Solar Plexus Chakra Affirmations To Use**

Most affirmations are usually meant to enable you to help your confidence. In this way, practically any positive sentence you make about yourself can lessen blockages in your solar plexus territory.

I have a list as usual, but you can structure specific expressions that speak to that nagging issue you have with your solar plexus chakra. You should try at least one of the following:

- I am full of inward harmony and confidence
-

- I have high confidence and I always think about myself in the best light possible
- I have control over my reaction to situations. I have self-control
- I don't need to be responsible for everything in my life
- I am powerful and I am OK with that
- I'm eager, competent, and prepared to meet my goal
- I feel motivated to seek after my goal
- I remove myself from negative past encounters
- I realize I am beautiful, great and competent
- I forgive myself for my mistakes, and I choose to learn from them

While you do this, remember you can switch it up! There are no rules but your rules. Tell yourself what you are, and watch as you become it.

Chapter Eight

The Heart Chakra

As you have already guessed, the heart chakra is associated with your ability for affection and empathy. This chakra is the fourth chakra, and is called **Anahata,** which is Sanskrit for "unbroken." It is sometimes portrayed as an extension between the psyche, body, and soul.

When your heart chakra is very aligned, you will most likely offer compassion to other people, be sincerely open, and appreciate an intense feeling of internal peace. You won't be afraid of how you feel any more because you would be able to relate with all things at a heart level.

Anything that has nothing to do with love can negatively affect your Anahata. A painful experience, self-loathing or a bad break up.

Physical Location: Directly over the heart.

Component: Air

Color: Green.

Signs of a Blocked Heart Chakra: When the heart chakra is blocked or misaligned, you'll have problems identifying with other people. You might be less caring or less compassionate than you usually are, and you'll have a hard time expressing your feelings. Your trust issues will hit the roof, and you'll feel frustrated and disappointed. It's not the end of the world, you are not simply cold-hearted, it just means your heart chakra is out of place. I am here to help you make it right again.

What Is The Root Chakra Responsible For?

You should see the heart chakra as a sort of extension between feelings, and spirituality, which means the Anahata is sometimes the most significant of all the chakras. The heart chakra is linked with the majority of the following:

- Your ability for sympathy.

- The intensity with which you can feel for someone else.
- Self-love
- Your ability to be passionate.
- How peaceful and calm you feel.
- Self-knowledge.

The point is, when your heart chakra is properly adjusted and completely open, you are a humane, loving, giving person. You feel completely generous with your emotions. This doesn't mean you get to be a public doormat, however.

Having a balanced heart chakra also implies understanding boundaries and knowing where to set yours. This means zero toxic relationships because toxic people bring toxic energy. During this blissful period, you will have a better handle on your own emotions because you can understand them now.

Then again, a blocked heart chakra can be caused by anything in life sincerely harmful to your feelings, or simply does not like you.

Side effects of a blocked Heart Chakra.

Each chakra becomes crooked sometimes or create

blockages. These blockages are very normal and can be major or minor, and will dependably lead you to feeling physically or emotionally shaky. Blocked heart chakra symptoms include:

- Lack of passion
- Irritable personality.
- Increased blood pressure.
- Trouble confiding in others.
- Absence of compassion.
- A sleeping disorder

There will be times when you don't know precisely what has turned out badly with your heart chakra, but luckily for you, healing your chakras doesn't always require that you know the reason. All things considered, there are some basic reasons why you may need to take a shot at fixing your heart chakra.

- Troublesome connections should be the first thing to go. Every toxic relationship in your life has to end. They don't even need to be romantic. Some friendships are just as poisonous. That toxic ex? Trash. That toxic
-

- coworker? Trash. That toxic family member? Try to fix things, if not...Trash.
- You may be recovering from a bad break up or a one-sided relationship where your affection didn't seem to be returned. Any of these problems can mean you need to start rehearsing heart chakra workouts.

What's more, in case you're trying to bury a truth about yourself, this kind of emotional suppression can push the heart chakra out of place. You need to come clean with yourself, so you can get back into alignment, and return to being love.

How to unblock your heart chakra

Opening chakras can turn out to be natural after you learn straightforward activities that encourage healing. I'm sure we can all agree that all-round knowledge of the chakras is important. For now though, let us focus on the heart chakra, before we move on to the others.

By practicing these heart chakra healing methods, you can **finally** let passion know it's totally okay to stop by. An open heart chakra will allow you to better comprehend and address your issues, and to offer love to other people. You may also find you are no longer afraid of your feelings or feelings in general. You also get better at tolerating and moving past your feelings without having to repress them.

As a little something extra, an open heart chakra is really helpful for all types of chakra healing. At the point when your psyche, body, and spirituality are in sync, it's simpler to make changes in your entire body. Interested in how to unblock and realign the heart chakra? Read on to know!

1. Heart Chakra Stones And Jewelry

Chakra stones are anything but difficult to use. Some of the time, you could simply wear them on yourself, for example, in a neckband or stud. Or you could consider holding one during a heart chakra meditation as well. We'll see how to do that sort of healing in a minute.

The heart chakra color test tell us that green is the color most intently connected with this chakra. Which means, don't be surprised if you end up looking like a tree after you're done wearing all the heart chakra stones. *Because trees have green leaves and chakra stones ha- ...Never mind.*

- **Jade**: This semi-valuable heart chakra stone is also called **dreamer's stone** and is connected to emotional adjustment, and healing. This stone has been used to mend broken hearts over generations. You can also profit by concentrating on this stone when you are dealing with a misfortune or spiritual damage.

- **Green calcite**: This stone is traditionally used for absorbing and trashing negative energy, and that makes it your best choice when you are thinking that it's difficult to feel compassion. This stone will help you to concentrate on healing from lack of empathy. Bring some love and light into your life with this beautiful stone.

- **Green aventurine**: The beautiful **stone of opportunity.** This stone is linked to energy, imperativeness, and motivation. It is said to help with troublesome feelings and emotional roadblocks. It is a love crystal that also helps with skin issues. This stone is for you is you need some luck right about now.

- **Rose quartz**: Heart chakra gems aren't constantly green. This pink stone is now and again called the "heart stone" and is said to attract all kinds of love and enable you to regain balance.

2. **Heart Chakra Meditation And Yoga**

Techniques

Meditation is good for your chakras and your chakras are good for you. If you ever need to unblock your heart chakra and you can't seem to find any of the stones, that's fine. Meditation works perfectly, too. However, you have to be consistent with it. You must do it every day.

Straightforward activities like deep breathing and internal body scanning are all in the chakra business. However, there are specific heart chakra meditation systems you can use when you sense a blockage coming on. Here is the best among the heart chakra meditation techniques for beginners:

- Locate a happy place. A relaxing spot where you won't be bothered.
- Sit and breathe in through your nose and out through your mouth for a couple of minutes. Feel your body relaxing as you do this.
- While your eyes are still closed, imagine that you're attracting a lot of energy up through your body towards the heart, beginning at the base of the spine and moving upwards.

- Picture that energy transforming into a large green ball of energy sitting at the center of the heart chakra. As you breathe in and breathe out, see that ball. Watch it grow brighter and brighter.
- Concentrate on tuning into feelings of adoration for yourself as well as other people, giving the energy a chance to flow through your entire body. Come out of the meditation after 3-6 minutes or when you feel ready.

Like I have said before, note that all types of yoga are useful for unblocking chakras. Simply adding 10 minutes of yoga to the beginning or end of your day will reduce chakra blockage.

3. Chakra Foods List And Diet Suggestions

While food may not be the main thing that rings a bell when you consider working with chakras, what you eat really affects these energy centers. As I mentioned earlier, all fresh and natural foods are great for all chakras, but this chapter is strictly about the heart chakra, so we'll be looking at foods that concern that particular energy center. After reading this, you can make adjustments to your eating routine to suit this specific chakra that is causing you problems.

Here are probably the best heart chakra foods and fruits to turn to when you feel blocked or uneasy:

- **Green foods**: Anything green is connected to the heart chakra. This implies you can't turn out badly with fixings like kale, limes, green ringer peppers, spinach, and green apples. These can help balance your heart.
- **Warm soups**: A hearty and rich soup can renew your passion and help you heal from past injuries. There is some narrative proof that soups can help recovery from illnesses. *So, err, soup, anyone?*
- **Vitamin C:** Finally, squeezed orange, strawberries, and different natural products that contain a lot of vitamin C can help the heart chakra. You can combine these organic products with green vegetables to make a lovely smoothie!

4.   **Heart Chakra Affirmations To Use**

By now, you should be used to affirmations, because they are fantastic for disposing of old, suffocating convictions and building confidence. That being said, it won't hurt to add some new affirmations to your daily schedule or tweak a portion of your old ones.

This is because you can get your heart to literally listen to you by using certain words and expressions. You can use these affirmations as a preventive measure or when you feel a blockage coming on. Here are some examples:

- I pick pure joy, empathy, and love
- I love myself genuinely, and offer a similar love to other people
- My heart is free from every one of the injuries of the past.
- I know my own feelings, and I acknowledge them
- I pardon others, and I pardon myself
- I always satisfy my heart's craving
- I am available to love, and be loved
- I give love unconditionally and it brings me peace and happiness
- My heart chakra is open, and I am well
- I make steady, beautiful relationships that are beneficial to me

Chapter Nine

THE THROAT CHAKRA

The throat chakra is the fifth chakra which is sometimes called Vishuddha. **Vishuddha** is Sanskrit, which translates to "pure." It is in charge of self-expression and truth. This chakra deals with how you express yourself to the world through your words. Your truth, responsibility and sense of humor are connected to this energy center.

When your throat chakra is properly aligned, you will feel ready to say what you mean, to say the truth without hurting others. Basically, you will be candid without being hurtful.

Troublesome situations with communication can move the throat chakra out of place. For instance, a tough meeting or an awful conversation.

Physical Location: Inside the throat.

Component: Ether

Color: Blue.

Signs of a Blocked Throat Chakra: A blocked throat chakra mainly shows a powerlessness to say what you truly need to say. You may feel like you're stuck clutching secrets or you may accept that individuals would prefer not to hear your thoughts, or that you can't just find the correct words for your emotions.

A little blockage means you just battle with self-expression at work, or with a specific person, while a huge one means you always feel frustrated when you even think of communication. Physically, a blocked throat chakra may give neck irritation, hormone imbalance and other throat tissues.

What Is The Throat Chakra Responsible For?

Now that you know the response to the question "what is a chakra?", we can move on to take a look at the effect of the throat chakra specifically. Also called the **Vishuddha**, this chakra rests inside your neck, directly at the throat. It personally deals with all your self-expression, so it influences and is influenced by *everything* to do with communication.

The throat chakra can affect the majority of the following:

- Your emotional truth
- The authenticity of your life
- How well you handle struggle or conflict.
- The nature of your relationships
- Your capacity to be heard
- Your awareness of your needs

When your throat chakra is open, you'll be incredible at making yourself understood. You'll have the option to say what you truly need to say and people will listen. You'll realize what you need, and have the ability to express yourself in a way that will make people want to listen to you more. This kind of alignment in the throat chakra can affect both your own and other lives, as great communication is important in every meaningful relationship.

But when the throat chakra becomes blocked and unhappy, blocked throat chakra signs start to show. This can happen whenever you think it's hard to speak with others, or whenever somebody makes you feel like they're not listening to you.

Side effects of a Blocked Throat Chakra

Having problems with your throat chakra is not abnormal and will happen every now and then, even when you become a Reiki master. It is expected to have throat chakra problems, but the most important thing is to know how to handle them when they come.

Symptoms of a blocked throat chakra include:

- Trouble saying what you need to
- A sore throat
- Coming up short on the vocabulary to express your feelings
- Hormone imbalances
- Having a feeling that you're clutching a lot of secrets
- Neck problems
- A feeling that individuals don't have a clue about the genuine you

All chakras can create minor blockages that are difficult to see, so don't beat yourself up when you see you can't generally pinpoint the source. That being said, it's good to know a portion of the triggers for a blocked throat chakra just in case.

The primary examples have one thing or the other to do with painful memories of communication, like an argument at a restaurant or at work or with a close friend. You can also block your throat chakra by not expressing yourself. I know this may sound conflicting because self-expression can lead to arguments and hurtful words, but not when you do it right. Express yourself with the aim to be understood not the aim to hurt anyone, no matter how tempting it may seem.

How to unblock your throat chakra

Chakra healing can sound complicated and impossible, and you might think it will take a steady commitment before you can start properly opening chakras to treat blockages, but fortunately for everyone, chakra activities are not even as close to difficult as you may think. You can learn them all in a single weekend, and their simplicity does not make them any less powerful.

Whenever you make the choice of fixing your throat chakra, you raise your odds of having an upbeat lifestyle. You will see insane upgrades in your communication skills. This can be very liberating if you ask me.

Mending your throat chakra can also cut off memories of disappointment at work or with friends, giving you a chance to discover what you truly want to say and say it! *You will finally stop having to lie so much*.

1.   Throat Chakra Stones And Jewelry

Since the chakra hues test revealed to us the official color for the throat chakra is blue, any blue precious stones would help the throat chakra. The thought here is straightforward. You should simply wear throat chakra stones, or even carry these chakra stones in your palm or purse. This direct approach will keep you aware of the throat chakra, and unblock it.

- **Lapis Lazuli**: This semi-valuable stone is also called the "**stone of truth**" or "**stone of the gods.**" It demonstrates honesty in all its forms, and should be used when trying to have a deep discussion. It is the best stone for temperamental children, because they just can't communicate properly. Therefore, it's a perfect stone to use when you're attempting to communicate all the more genuinely.

- **Aquamarine gemstone**: One of the most notable throat chakra gems, the aquamarine gem has constantly spoken to boldness and truth. You may float towards this one if you have especially huge communication issues in cozy relationships.

- **Amazonite**: A delightful turquoise stone, amazonite is trusted to protect you against doubt. All you need to do is wear it as a necklace or bracelet if you find you can't speak up out of fear of judgement.

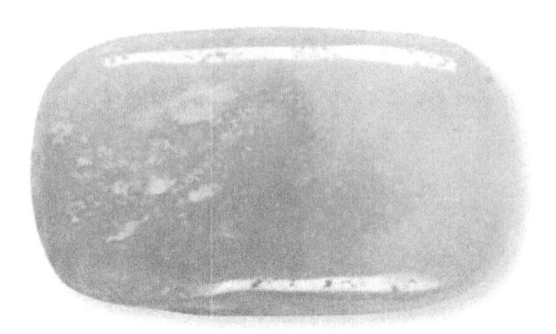

- **Turquoise**: Another semi-valuable stone, turquoise is connected to boosting trust in communication.

2. Throat Chakra Meditation And Yoga

Anybody can get chakra healing manuals for learners. This means even if you've never really tried yoga, you won't have an issue. I advise you do your throat chakra meditation every day for 12 minutes, even though it doesn't really matter, because you will see results whether you practice for 5 minutes every day or 10. The trick is consistency.

This is what to do:

- Sit down in a comfortable seat in a calm room. Close your eyes. Breathe in and breathe out multiple times, as deeply as possible. Breathe in through your nose, out through your mouth.
- Beginning at the highest point of your head, you'll need to feel through your body with your mind. Watch your muscles relax as you do so.
- When you've done this for your entire body, picture a turning ball in any shade of blue (the throat chakra color). See it sitting at the center of your throat, and imagine it sparkling.

- See the blue circle getting greater and greater, concentrating on a feeling of honesty and relaxation in the throat.
- Allow the energy to scatter through your body, and after that, open your eyes when you're prepared.

Then, probably the best throat chakra postures are the **child cobra**, **bear stand**, and **bolstered fish**. You can discover simple photos of these on the Internet.

3. Chakra Foods List And Diet Suggestions

Here we'll discuss chakra foods that deal with openness and honesty. You can unblock your chakra by eating these foods even without daily meditation or chakra stones, but for brilliant results, it's better to combine them. As a little something extra, these foods are particularly in line with - generally speaking - **smart dieting**. Consider whole grain foods like dark colored rice, plus low or zero sugar consumption. However, there are exact dietary changes you can make to unblock particular chakras. Here are examples of the best throat chakra mending foods:

- **Blueberries**: In light of their obvious blue tint, blueberries are among the strongest fruits for the throat chakra. They can be blended with blackberries and coconut to make a fantastic and nourishing smoothie for the throat. Take a shot at it when you realize you will have a difficult discussion!
- **Fruits**: Apples, oranges and every other natural product that develops on trees are connected with the throat chakra. Some people say this is because these fruits symbolize truth and legitimacy. They literally only drop from the tree when it is time to be eaten.
- **Different spices**: Add salt, lemongrass, or ginger to meals when you're attempting to heal the throat chakra. These will help with clear self-expression.

4. **Throat Chakra Affirmations**

Whenever you state an affirmation that you mean and feel as truth, you're promoting a solid throat chakra. Awesome! This implies you don't generally need to make a special effort to create throat chakra affirmations. Just sticking to an everyday practice is enough. I have a list, as usual.

- I can express my feelings, regardless of what they are
- My voice is significant in this world
- I respect my real voice, and I make use of it
- I am constantly understood by others
- I am a good audience and an even better communicator
- Others hear me
- When I talk, my words are straightforward but not hurtful
- I know the correct words to use in all circumstances
- I don't doubt my words
- I speak my mind effortlessly

When you say these affirmations, it is best to look into a mirror and watch your lips move as you do - although that is just icing on an already perfect cake.

Chapter Ten

THE THIRD EYE CHAKRA

The third eye Chakra is the sixth chakra. It is also called **Ajna,** which is Sanskrit for "perceive." It is an incredible energy source when it is working properly. It decides your instinct, your arrangement with the Universe, and your capacity to see the master plan throughout everyday life.

When you have an open third eye chakra, you are good at getting signs. You should trust in your premonitions and plan as you are directed by your third eye chakra. However, the third eye can be blocked when somebody is making you question your instincts or gut feeling, or when you decide logic makes more sense than that nagging feeling you have.

Physical Location: In the midpoint of your forehead.

Component: Extra-sensory perception.

Color: Indigo.

Related Animal: Black Antelope.

Signs of Blocked a Third Eye Chakra: When your third eye chakra is blocked, you may feel lost most of the time. You stop trusting your instincts and feel there's probably no good reason for whatever it is you're doing. You will also feel greatly indecisive;

Buy shoes, don't buy shoes, buy shoes, don't buy shoes.

A few people consider this to be an emotional loss of motion. You could also have trouble sleeping and battle with change.

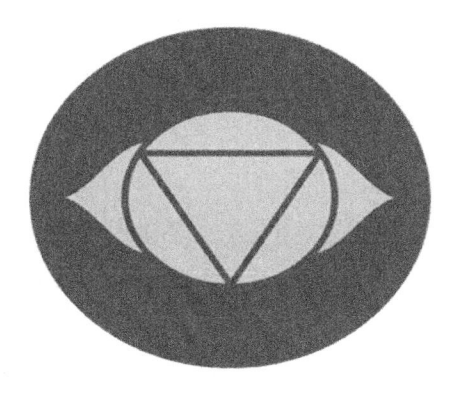

What Is The Third Eye Chakra Responsible For?

The third eye chakra (or the Ajna chakra) is located right on your forehead, and it is associated with your spirituality and ability to perceive.

Given the Ajna's importance, the third eye influences (and is influenced by) the majority of the following things:

- Your capacity to have clear premonitions.
- Your feeling of the master plan throughout everyday life.
- Your sense of justice.
- Balancing feelings and reason.
- Whether or not you feel you are moving forward in life.

In this way, when your third eye is open, you will use the emotions and sense of reason to settle on major choices throughout your day. You will trust in your very own instincts, and you will be open to realizing that you're experiencing your goal. When you practice third eye chakra healing, you can see an obvious change in your connection with your general surroundings, and in your ability to be cautious.

When you're managing a third eye chakra blockage, you can begin to get negative third eye chakra side effects. This can happen when something makes you question your instincts, or when something gives you reasons to back up and rethink your life's goal.

Manifestations of a Blocked Third Eye Chakra

Nobody experiences life without chakra blockages. Literally no one. So don't stress if you have to fix your third eye chakra more than once. What matters is that you can notice these symptoms, and begin work on them as soon as possible. Some symptoms of a blocked third eye chakra include:

- Absence of confidence in your life's goal.
- Finding your life or work unimportant.
- Feeling inconsequential.
- Feeling highly suspicious of everything and everyone.
- Feeling uncertain or indecisive.

Third eye blockages can also trigger a variety of **inconvenient** physical signs such as:

- Insane headaches.
- Sinus infections.
- Back and leg discomfort.
- Eye problems

Everybody has different triggers that point out the need for third eye healing. However, I think it is helpful to know about probably the most well-known reasons for blockages in the third eye.

For instance, when somebody makes fun of your job or energy, this can push the third eye chakra out of alignment. Also, experiencing a major health issue, losing a family member or close friend, a divorce, or losing a job. Even simply moving into another phase of your life (for example around a huge birthday) affects your third eye chakra, because you're new to the territory and you're not sure what to do.

How to unblock your third eye chakra

Third eye healing isn't as rocket science-y as it may sound. While the third eye opening can be considered to be very important, the kinds of methods that open the third eye chakra are shockingly basic.

1.   Third Eye Chakra Stones And Jewelry

There is a chakra color test that tells us what color belongs to what chakra, and for the third eye chakra, the key color is purple. This gives you a pretty good idea of what stones go with this chakra.

The idea is to look for accessories carrying purple gemstones, and wear them whenever you have to unblock the third eye chakra. Or you could just buy bigger third eye precious stones that will sit nicely in your home or in the palm of your hand, enabling you to squeeze on them and focus on them when you have to keep your third eye chakra open.

The absolute best third eye stones are:

- **Purple fluorite**: This semi-valuable diamond is also called the "**genius stone,**" and should elevate honed instinct and to clear up tangled thoughts. It's a perfect third eye chakra gem when you're attempting to settle on a decision and need to dispose of unnecessary distractions.

- **Amethyst**: An acclaimed and wonderful valuable stone, amethyst is usually associated with third eye pain alleviation and other types of healing. A few people sometimes use it to represent wisdom.

- **Dark Obsidian**: Another famous individual from the third eye precious stones gathering, dark obsidian advances balance between feeling and reason.

2. Third Eye Chakra Yoga and Meditation

Meditation may be one of the first things that rings a bell when you think about the question "What is a chakra?" Anyhow, third eye meditation is only one of the many approaches to take when taking a shot at opening this chakra. Fortunately, there are a lot of chakra meditation procedures for learners as well, so don't stress because you've never attempted meditation or yoga. Here's one to begin with:

- Sit still and close your eyes. Breathe in and breathe out multiple times, gradually and deeply.
- Concentrate on the area of the third eye chakra, envision a violet circle of energy inside your temple. Keep in mind, purple is the third eye chakra's color.
- As you keep on breathing gradually and deeply, picture the purple chunk of energy getting greater and hotter. As it does, envision it cleansing cynicism from your body.
- Consider yourself retaining the third eye chakra's energy. Now, allow yourself to feel it everywhere.

- Open your eyes when you feel prepared.

As you may have thought, yoga is also very useful when figuring out how to adjust your chakras. Third eye yoga postures include **child's pose** and the **falcon pose**. You can check the Internet later for pictures and recordings that will help you through these positions. Prepare to start using your third eye!

3. Third Eye Chakra Foods List And Diet Suggestions.

Usually, fundamental chakra foods (that is, ones that help all chakras) are generally healthy. For instance, all natural products, vegetables, unsaturated fats and whole grain substances will in general make your chakras happy and in turn, make you happy.

However, there are very specific third eye chakra fruits and foods, and adding them to your day by day diet can avoid or reduce blockages. Remember the following:

Chocolate (dark) : If you are a fan of dark chocolate, don't hesitate to have as much as you need when you're attempting to open the third eye! It is said to help improve mental lucidity and increase focus. It is an extraordinary source of magnesium, which reduces stress in you. As a little something extra, it promotes the production of serotonin, also called the happy hormone.

Anything purple: Given that purple is the third eye's color, every single purple food or fruit is automatically a third eye chakra food. The absolute best are red grapes, eggplants, blackberries, purple cabbage, and blueberries.

Omega-3: Foods that contain a lot of omega-3 can upgrade intellectual capacity while helping to keep your third eye chakra open. Great examples are chia seeds, pecans, sardines, and salmon.

4. Third Eye Chakra Affirmations

When trying to create affirmations for the third eye, you need to concentrate on your gut instinct, spirituality, and your fundamental feeling of direction. Here are a few examples you can attempt. Don't hesitate to switch them up until they feel right for you.

- I know how to settle on the correct choices, and I do so effortlessly
- I follow the lead of my internal instructor
- I am following my true path
- I listen to my instincts and I realize they will lead me to my goal
- I live each day following my life's goal

- I trust in the direction that my third eye gives me
- My possibilities are limitless!
- I am an instinctive individual, and I understand what is directly for me
- It in my interest to pursue the direction of my third eye
- My third eye is open and prepared to see my goal

Chapter Eleven

THE CROWN CHAKRA

In Sanskrit, the crown chakra is called the **Sahasrara,** which means "thousand petaled." This chakra is what connects you to all things spiritual, and etheric.

Physical Location: The highest point of the head.

Component: Thought.

Color: Violet.

Related Animal: Eagle

Signs of Blockage: If your chakra has been misaligned or blocked, you may very well notice a decrease in general energy or inspiration. Physically, a blocked crown chakra can occur as issues with physical coordination or good ol' fashioned migraines. Talk about a spiritual hangover! Yikes!

What Is The Crown Chakra Responsible For?

The crown chakra (or Sahasrara chakra) is the

seventh chakra, and it sits at the highest point of your head. This specific chakra's importance is about spiritual availability.

The thing about the crown chakra or sahasrara, is it's the most elevated chakra, and it can affect (or be affected by) anything on the following list

- How much beauty you can find in your general surroundings.

- Inspiration to achieve objectives.
- Your capacity to discover harmony.
- Your energy levels.
- Your self-esteem.
- Whether or not you have soothing rest.

At the point when your crown chakra is appropriately adjusted and completely open, you will encounter a ton of joy throughout the day. You'll feel appreciative, alive and like your days are loaded with delight. With basic crown chakra healing methods, you can improve your spiritual mindfulness and start to appreciate the little snapshots of beauty life brings to the table.

Then again, when you're bothered with a crown chakra blockage, you're probably going to experience upsetting crown chakra symptoms which means you can end up baffled, exhausted, melancholic, and even bored.

How to unblock your Crown Chakra

Now we all know the response to the big question "what is the crown chakra?" we can take a look at the best chakra practices for the Sahasrara.

There are way developed strategies for the crown chakra you can learn in time on the off chance that you wish to. However, the easiest is pretty much the best. You see, when looking into how to adjust chakras for learners, you'll likely find practices that will work well for you for a long, long time. But for now, we'll concentrate on four specifically, which are all effectively fused into regular day-to-day life, and require no unnecessary preparation.

While all the methods can be performed individually, you can try to combine two or more methods together. For instance, stones can be used during meditation practice, and yoga can be performed while saying affirmations.

1. Crown Chakra Stones And Jewelry

As indicated by the standard chakra colors test, the crown chakra is related to the color violet, but it also has connections to clear stones and gems.

With regards to using chakra stones for healing, you have a lot of options. You can either wear crown chakra stones in neckbands, studs, and wrist trinkets, or you can just easily hold them or focus on them. *Easy peasy*!

To begin, try at least one of these crown chakra precious stones:

Clear quartz: A crystalline mineral connected to improving energy, you can use clear quartz to support your spiritual attunement. It is an especially decent decision when you're hoping to get clarity on what you need from life. *The stone is literally clear.*

- **Sugilite**: Sometimes known as an adoration stone, this lavender gem is better used for spiritual stuff and for guarding you against cynicism.

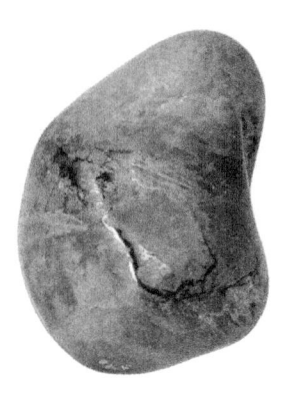

- **Selenite**: Another generally clear mineral, selenite is a beautiful stone that is said to help open the crown chakra as well as the third eye chakra. It very well may be helpful in pushing you past stagnation and help you go forward.

2. Crown Chakra Yoga and Meditation

All meditation practices are useful for keeping the seven chakras open and balanced. Reflection promotes mindfulness, enthusiasm, and relaxation. Also, there are chakra reflection procedures for beginners that objective each chakra. Like the crown chakra for example.

- Sit with your back straight and your feet on the floor. Close your eyes.
- Put your hands in your lap and turn your palms to the sky. This position is known as the "mudra" and gives you energy.
- Shut your eyes and breathe in through your nose, then out through your mouth.
- Envision a lotus at the highest point of your head. As you keep on breathing gradually and equally, see the lotus petals spreading out to reveal to you a brilliant violet light - the crown chakra color.

- Picture the light getting more and more splendid, as it warms the crown of your head.
- Give that glow a chance to spread downwards all through your entire body.

- Following 5-10 minutes, open your eyes and sit still for a couple of minutes.

3.   Chakra Foods List And Diet Suggestions

The most celebrated chakra foods are common, healthy kinds that advance general health. Consider fresh and natural vegetables and organic products, darker rice, darker bread and warm soups, for instance. These foods help open up your chakra and promote good physical health.

In the future, when you're focusing on one chakra over the others, it's helpful to look to foods that have a customary association with that chakra. For the crown chakra, the majority of the following help to keep it open and responsive:

- **Violet fruits**: Eggplant and red grapes are perfect examples, as they're tuned in to the fundamental color of the crown chakra. Passionfruit is another superb alternative.
- **Ginger**: Although not purple, this zest is said to have purifying advantages, and it can advance spiritual clarity.

- **Natural teas**: On the subject of lucidity, homegrown teas can reduce blockages in the crown chakra. Peppermint is likely the best choice, and it has the special reward of fixing up your stomach if need be.

It's also important to note that since the crown chakra is simply spiritual, a few specialists figure the avoidance of specific foods or fruits can could really help too. Basically, whenever you cut back on greasy or sugary substances that contain zero nutrients, you're fixing up your crown chakra.

4. **Crown Chakra Affirmations To Use**

If you aren't already using some daily affirmations, now is an extraordinary time to begin!

Words are a notable strategy for adjusting the chakras. Every one of them mean to support certainty, and since the crown chakra is associated with confidence, then it makes perfect sense that affirmations go a long way in helping mend the crown chakra. These are my absolute best:

- I am always my most astounding self

- I am sensitive to the celestial energy of the universe
- We are all on this planet to have a kind of effect
- I know my very own truth and I live by it
- Today I am available to divine direction
- Affectionately, I radiate light that pulls in other people who will bring love into my life
- I see the beauty in life and I grasp it
- I am love, I am light, and I am euphoria
- At the present time, I am content, happy and certain about my value
- I am at one with my general surroundings

The right words have a ton to do with individual confidence, so don't hesitate to take a shot at giving your chakra a personal boost are various occasions of the day.

Chapter Twelve

TYPES OF REIKI SYSTEMS

Reiki is an arrangement of complete recovery; a personal journey; an adventure of self-improvement; or each of the three joined together. Despite the fact Reiki was presented by Dr. Mikao Usui, numerous varieties have improved upon his method.

Today, the conventional Reiki isn't the main elective drug. There are numerous different sorts of Reiki that can also be used for healing. I mean, think about it. If you're a professional Reiki healer, and you constantly give Reiki energy to other people, doesn't it make sense to discover or stumble upon some other method in route?

Most likely, this is the reason numerous methods and strategies for Reiki exist these days. In fact, these kinds of Reiki have turned out to be various schools which have their own ideas about using the Reiki energy.

From the original school of Reiki, different bosses and professionals have made their own system. Reiki works quite well with back rubs, directing, nursing, precious stones, hypnosis, fragrance based treatment, and so on, to help the healing procedure. The difference between various methods could be because of various symbols and methods that regularly result into various sorts of energy. Let's take a look at them:

- **Ancient Egyptian Reiki**

Reiki, as we all know, is used to mend individuals with its energy vibrations everywhere throughout the world. It is common in various cultures, and Ancient Egyptian Reiki is just as common.

Old Reiki healing of Egypt is, in truth, a particular type of Reiki that is still very available for the patients. It uses a very unique system, which is not the same as basic Reiki, but has somehow demonstrated extremely great results for every time I've used it.

In Egypt, the specialists had been rehearsing systems of Reiki since the time of the Pharaohs. Customary Reiki gets energy from a higher power, while Ancient Egyptian Reiki takes this energy and controls it, transforming it into solid vibrations which eventually become healing energy.

The main difference between Ancient Egyptian Reiki and conventional Reiki lies in the way that the former controls the forces of the Earth. Since the beginning of time, Egyptians have constantly revered and worshiped the Earth for what it has given to humanity. The idea of energy from it is, by all accounts, very normal for them. Egyptian Reiki uses the forces of Earth, Air, Fire, Water and Spirit to heal, open chakras and balance their patients. It can likewise combine radiant energies and the use of precious stones.

Plus, patients often get the opportunity to get the hang of healing systems like sound vibration healing, musical breathing, and so on in this type of Reiki. With this knowledge, don't you agree Ancient Egyptian Reiki is surely one of the best and most efficient type of Reiki ever created?

Another extraordinary component of Egyptian Reiki is 'negative energy channelling.' This system has the ability to cleanse negative energies from the patient during a Reiki healing session. It is very helpful for the general population who are sincerely troubled or stressed. A lot of people depend on this method to reduce their emotional sufferings. Whenever performed normally, Ancient Egyptian Reiki is the best treatment for your spirituality.

Sekhem is a type of Ancient Egyptian Reiki. Sekhem has existed throughout the hundreds of years and was a big deal in the Temples of Ancient Egypt. Egypt was then the social center of civilization where everybody looked for insight and learning, and researchers came from all over the world to study in their sanctuaries, but few endured the difficult procedures of initiation into the brotherhood.

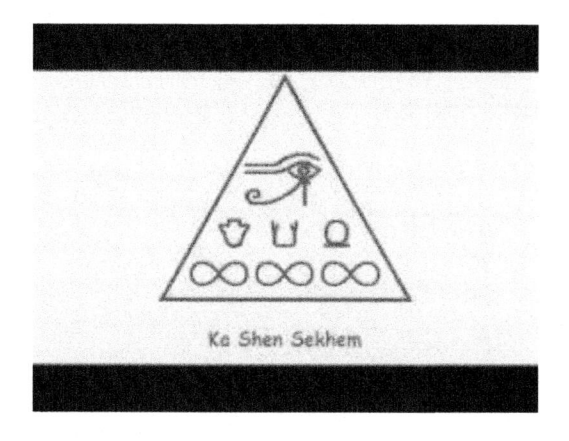

Some succeeded despite all that, and taught their lessons to their countries, generously showing others the craft of healing of magic. Throughout the years, the lessons changed as the instructors created and developed with their way of thinking, until every system had its own unmistakable feel and vibe.

The Sekhem energy is related with the Egyptian lion-headed Goddess Sekhmet, the Guardian and Protector of this energy. She is firmly connected with the star Sirus, the most brilliant star in the sky, and, as per legend, was available at the making of our universe.

This Goddess is the Bringer of Destruction and Healing, as she is both the Patroness of War and Healing Sciences, and in spite of the numerous fantasies of annihilation, she is additionally viewed as the Goddess of Regeneration and Healing. Sekhmet removes what is no longer useful to us, with the goal that we can expand on another establishment. Sekhmet also encourages us to change our lives and remove old faded methods which no longer serve us.

Sekhem translate to the *Power of Powers,* and is

associated with our very own strengthening for both healing and personal improvement. Once started, all our healing work makes an amazing improvement. In a spiritual sense, it is related to Chi, or Ki, or Prana.

Also, today there are numerous systems which are for the most part fundamentally the same as the Egyptian Reiki. Yet, they have their own unmistakable vibe. There is just one source really. All these are simply various methods of getting to it.

Although similar to Reiki, Sekhem is directed in an alternate manner, and has a way higher vibration. When you go to the temples, there are symbolic representations of the gods accepting healing sessions and initiations into various orders. These representations are carved into the walls of the temple . References have been made to Sekhem in the Egyptian Book of the Dead and in antique books found in the remnants of the sanctuaries and the pyramids.

How does Sekhem work?

Sekhem usually attempts to blend and adjust all parts of an individual's being – physical, mental, spiritual and emotional, while supporting the body's own normal healing procedures. Healing with the hands, where energy goes through the healer and all the way into the patient's energy field and body, has been used for generations to improve people's wellbeing.

All life creates an energy field around it. This field contains info about the physical structure of the individual; the condition of an individual's body, mind, spiritual, and emotional progress. A Sekhem healer can detect or check out this field and read this information, and when they do that, they direct Sekhem energy into the needed areas to promote healing and prosperity.

The physical body and the various layers of the energy field are connected by the chakras, which are live energy channels arranged along the spine. Every one of these channels or centers is connected to a specific layer in the spiritual body and to explicit organs in the physical body. They also identify with a person's mental state, for example, in relationships with our family and companions, as well as our confidence, our capacity to demonstrate genuine love, and our eagerness to express our feelings. Just like the individual layers of the energy field, each chakra contains information which can be accessed by a Sekhem professional.

In Sekhem healing, a person is viewed as a spiritual system with the physical body at the center. Despite that, a Sekhem healer would work all the more specifically on the aura, because sickness initially starts as a blockage in one of the spiritual centers or layers. In Sekhem, healing is considered to be as a two-way process. It is a method for supporting an individual during their own healing voyage.

Sekhem used 3-D symbols, which are connected to the art of the pyramids. This energy is basically unconditional love in its purest form. The symbols provide access to dimensional gateways. In healing sessions, the professional will put their hands on or close to the body and pass the Sekhem energy to the recipient.

It is good for pressure relief, quickens healing, advances mindfulness, prevents sickness, and detoxifies the body. It treats numerous conditions without being invasive.

- **Angelic Reiki**

As everyone knows, angels are creatures who live outside the laws of the physical and handle the whole working of the Universe. At the point when their direction is joined with the healing specialty of Reiki, the energy system of any individual or gathering can be seen in the most amazing way. This impact can be made on physical, spiritual and mental level.

Angelic Reiki is literally a blend of the hands-on methodology of Reiki, with the healing forces of the Angelic kingdom. It loosens up the soul and mind. Like the customary Reiki, Angelic Reiki likewise is useful for self-healing and distance healing, with symbols being the common denominator for both.

Angelic Reiki is not the same as others in the fact that angelic vibration helps the normal vibration while connecting the professional and recipient to their spirit energy. Unlike other types of Reiki, the attunements are finished by the holy messengers themselves in Angelic Reiki. Its symbols, alongside different things, are drawn unto the body while the healing session is being performed. For the recipient, this procedure will bring change, and you will definitely let go of old baggage, worry, and pain.

- **Kundalini Reiki**

Most people view Kundalini Reiki as one of the least complex forms or Reiki, as well as one of the best. Kundalini Reiki is quite similar to the normal Reiki, but is a bit more uncomplicated. *I'll explain.*

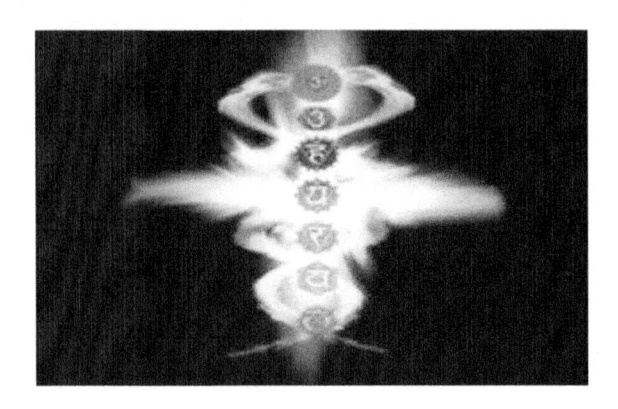

The energy being used here is called the **Kundalini energy or Kundalini fire**. Most people see the energy as very dominant and potent, but like other energies, it has a source. Some higher power that is usually accessed by Reiki masters.

Most people say they feel livelier and happier after a Kundalini Reiki session. The major difference between the Normal Reiki sessions and the Kundalini Reiki sessions is that during a typical Kundalini session, the energy is usually centered around the root chakra, after which it spreads to other parts of the body, unlike with the normal Reiki session where the energy is usually transferred to the affected part of the body.

- **Karuna Reiki**

This is one of the forms of Reiki healing. It was created by a man named William Rand. This system is a byproduct of Tera-mai, which is a different system of healing altogether.

Dear old Mr. William borrowed the symbols of Tera-Mai and studied them. While he did that, he realised the energy shifted and became focused on the heart, so he named it **Karuna**, which literally means **compassionate.**

Everyone is somehow connected to each other, and this explains why we can't help but be compassionate. Karuna Reiki explains that we heal others while we heal ourselves. *How beautiful is that?*

Karuna will motivate you to go around helping people and ending suffering. Karuna will make you give that last granola bar to the little boy on the street. It'll make you pay a visit to the orphanage to share your love with those beautiful children. When you further understand Karuna, you'll be better at healing others - who are just extensions of yourself.

Karuna Reiki is more defined than the traditional Reiki system. It has 8 treatment symbols and 4 master symbols

1. The first treatment symbol heals a person deeply and helps deal with guilt from the past. You don't have to worry anymore about Karma with this symbol.
2. The second symbol will set you free from all those negative things in your life that just won't let you see the truth. This will fix denial.
3. The third symbol deals with love. The unconditional kind.
4. The fourth symbol is usually used for conclusion.

The second set are more complicated than these four, and since that's beyond the scope of this book, I'll let you do that research on your own. Or maybe I'll write about it. We'll see.

- **Usui Reiki**

This system of Reiki is the original. It was founded by Mikao Usui, the original founder of Reiki healing. *I mentioned him somewhere earlier.*

Mikao Usui

Usui Reiki or Usui Ryoho is a system that uses natural methods of healing or the universal life force for growth and healing. This form of Reiki is very personal. It is used to fix emotional, mental, physical and spiritual issues.

Usui Reiki has been passed down from generation to generation by teachings, sharing stories or just plain treatments. It is not a healing method that can be learned from a book or scroll. If you're interested in becoming a Reiki master, you have to be properly

lectured by a master.

Oddly, it is easy to learn and can be used to fix a variety of problems mentally and physically.

A typical Reiki session involves the healer laying hands close to, but not on the body of the recipient, while energy flows into the patient's body. As the recipient, you may feel a lot of different things like I explained earlier - cold, heat, vibration, unusual heaviness, and so on. Or you may feel nothing. That's not unusual either.

A typical session which is 50- 80 minutes can relax muscles you didn't even know you had. It can make you feel emotionally light and mentally active.

Chapter Thirteen

REIKI AURA

On the surface or skin of every living being, there's some energy that surrounds them. More like a magnetic field but swap **magnet** for **energy.** This energy is called an **aura**. It does not just float around the surface of the body; some of it seeps into the body too.

The intensity of an aura is different for each person depending on a lot of reasons like mood, the environment, and so on. A typical aura has layers or levels. Each layer is connected to the next and previous, and has a specific frequency.

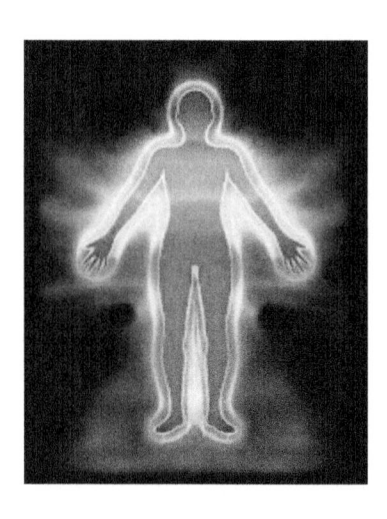

All the layers constantly affect the emotional, mental, physical, and spiritual state of a person, as well as the people around them. What I'm saying is that if one teeny tiny layer of your aura is wonky, your whole aura may get wonky too. The layers are connected to every chakra in the body. *Please don't make me explain chakras again.*

Aura levels and your corresponding needs

1) Physical level - Physical sensations. Simple physical comfort, pleasure, health.
2) Vital level - Rational mind. To understand the situation in a clear, linear, rational way.
3) The ethereal level - Emotions with respect to self. Self-acceptance and self-love.
4) piritual level - Divine mind, serenity. To be connected to divine mind and to understand the greater universal pattern.
5) Astral level - Relations with others. Loving interaction with friends and family.
6) Lower mental level - Divine will within. To align with the divine will within, to make a commitment to speak and follow the truth.
7) Higher mental level - Divine love, and spiritual ecstasy.

Aura colors and their meaning

Blue aura Unfortunately, blue isn't just blue. There is dark blue, light blue, turquoise blue, yada yada

yada. And each shade of blue means something in the aura world. *Dark blue* means psychic or clairvoyant. *Turquoise blue* means bad energy. If your aura is turquoise blue, it means you are empathic, and likely have attracted the negative energies of the people around you.

Red Aura *Bright red* is typically like the turquoise aura in relation to empathy. *Light red aura* means you're positive and full of energy! But people with this aura are good at using smiles to cover up a bucket load of tears. *Dark red* means bad energy or negative feelings. You need to let the past go.

Green aura *Light green* stands for healing and compassion. But people with this aura usually don't take part in things that don't particularly concern them. They'd rather not waste their time. This can be a good thing and a bad thing. *Dark green* represents negativity like other dark colours I mentioned. Anger and jealousy is usually associated with this aura. **Green-eyed monster!**

Pink aura When people think pink, they think soft, feminine, right? If you have a pink aura, you're not so different from people with a red aura. You're just purer. Like other aura, the pink aura has different shades. *Baby pink aura* means you're not materialistic. You don't care about Fendi, Lambos or Kylie Jenner. *Bright pink aura* represents a balance between the spiritual world and the material world. It is an updated baby pink version. *Dark pink aura* means you're slowly finding yourself on the path of negativity but you're still pink, so it's not too late to fix it.

White aura You guessed it! It represents purity. Not much talk there.

Purple aura If you have this aura, you probably just love love and relationships. This color is linked to the heart chakra which explains a lot.

Black aura First of all, this aura doesn't automatically scream evil. It might mean chaos and turmoil or just a blocked aura.

Yellow aura This aura has connections to life energy and the spleen. It is the color of intelligence, spiritual awakening, inspiration, creativity, joy and sheer happiness. Just like other auras, this one also has different shades that represent different things. *Light or pale yellow* represents spiritual and psychic awareness. Hope. Positivity. New ideas.

If you seem to be struggling to maintain control over a relationship or you have a major fear of not being in control, your aura is most definitely bright lemon-yellow. If it's a *shiny metallic gold,* you are full of inspiration, spirituality, and power. *Dark yellow or brown?* Students most likely have this aura because of the fatigue and excessive studying trying to cover the entire curriculum.

Gold aura This is the color of enlightenment and protection from a higher power. Whenever you see this aura is a person, know that he/she is protected by a divine power. It signifies wisdom, deep knowledge, spirituality, intuition, and divinity.

Chapter Fourteen

REIKI AND HEALING CRYSTALS

Crystals are beautiful naturally occurring stones with a lot of amazing properties and uses. Crystals are a big part of unorthodox medicine, a good example being Reiki. In one of the previous chapters, I explained how Reiki energy moves through the seven chakras in the body before these chakras, in turn, distribute this energy to areas of the body where they are needed.

These chakras are like passageways, and when there's a roadblock, energy won't be able to spread to necessary parts of the body. A million things can cause a chakra roadblock.

Some crystals happen to exist to unblock chakras, among other things. These crystals can be placed in the area of the chakra blockage during a Reiki session or held in the hand of the patient.

It's important to note that not all crystals unblock all chakras. Each chakra has its own specific set of crystals, so a third eye chakra gemstone cannot unblock your throat chakra. Mostly these gemstones are associated with the chakras by color except for a select few. We may have covered a few already, but I'm going to go over a few more attributes, okay?

Let's take a look shall we?

- **Aquamarine Crystal** Aquamarine is a big deal in the energy stone business and a great healing companion to Reiki. It is the stone for you if you are seeking courage, determination, strength, success and communication.

  Because it is an ocean stone, it provides calm to whoever possesses it. It is really useful during meditation or yoga for clarity, creativity and self-expression. Aquamarine is also believed to protect those who travel on water. Buy a bracelet or necklace with aquamarine crystals.

  This stone will help reduce anxiety and depression. It is a throat chakra crystal and it enhances speech and honesty. Aquamarine is an excellent stone for reaching the highest level of your spirituality while keeping yourself well-grounded at the same time.

- **Rhodonite Crystal**

    Rhodonite is a beautiful red stone that is linked to the heart chakra. This is used to treat emotional wounds and past scars and even physical wounds. However, when you have serious physical injuries, this stone won't stitch you up nicely, so tell a friend to get you an Uber cause honey, you need a **doctor**.

After you get medical care however, you can place the rhodonite gem on the area to speed up healing.

Rhodonite is the stone of love, empathy and

affection, being connected with the heart chakra and all. It maintains the balance between good and evil. When there's an issue of panic attack, abuse and dependency, use this stone.

- **Selenite Crystal** Selenite is a Crown chakra stone and is great for Reiki healing because of the many many ways it can be helpful to physical and spiritual health. It is sometimes called the **calming stone** because it is used to calm people during Reiki sessions or meditation.

In meditation, it reveals your inner truth and relaxes your troubled mind. It is used for mental enhancement, telepathy and astral projection. Selenite is a self-cleansing stone. Put selenite in your room to disperse negative energy.

- **Clear quartz** Clear quartz is a crown chakra crystal that deals with storage, absorption and regulation of energy.

This stone attracts negative energy and draws it out of our bodies and environments. It is a purification stone.

- **Amethyst Crystal** Amethyst is known to be very protective. It increases your energy to a level where negative energies cannot reach and hurt you. This stone is a protection stone with calming properties.

Use this stone during Reiki to create a beautiful combination of love and healing energies. Amethyst helps with sleeping problems, stress, migraines and paranoia.

- **Red jasper crystal**   Red jasper, a gem usually associated with the root chakra energy, is one of the most effective stones for the protection of your own energy system when you are surrounded by negative energies of any kind.

What's more, red jasper gives you the courage to speak up. It is a very helpful stone to have with you if you find yourself between a rock and a hard place. Red jasper can also heal your aura and balance out your energies by filtering the negative ones.

Whenever you are surrounded by a negative energy, red jasper will draw it out of the environment into itself. It will literally take the hit and most likely crack or split into pieces.

- **Tiger eye Crystal**   This beautiful stone is also known as the shape-shifting stone. It builds courage and stability. When you use this stone during a Reiki session, you will find your confidence has been given an immense boost. This is the gemstone of the solar plexus chakra, and we all know what this chakra is about, don't we?

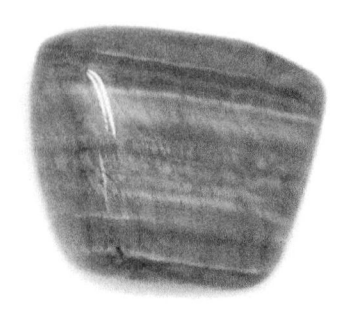

The tiger stone helps get rid of toxic feelings, fear, and self-doubt. *Try holding it through a horror movie... ha*!

If you find yourself drowning in self-doubt, hold this stone in your hand and imagine its energy flowing through your solar plexus chakra.

- **Bloodstone Crystal**   Bloodstone energy is the kind that hits you like a proper workout or a fun date. it's plain amazing! Bloodstone touches every single cell of your body so that you're not just living, you are **bursting with life**!

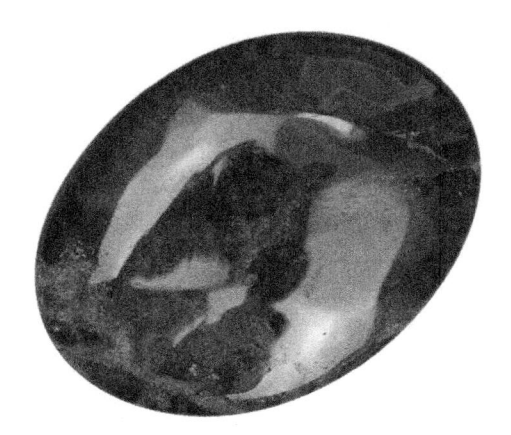

When you need a reminder of what gets your blood

racing **- in a good way -** in life, get in sync with the energy this stone. Bloodstone healing is all about getting you up and about. This is not a stone that allows you stay right where you are.

With this stone, time in your comfort zone is limited. You have to be on the go! If you're feeling lazy or just uninterested, bloodstone will snap you right out of it. This is particularly useful if you're taking on a new project.

This stone is a heart chakra stone as you may have already guessed, and it is used to open up the heart to feel and love again. This stone will give you the strength and courage to go back out there and start doing the things you love!

- **Flower Agate Crystal** Flower Agate is a brand-new stone all the way from Madagascar. Like a blossom tree, this gemstone will help you bloom into your greatest potential. This is a stone of transformation, new beginnings and growth.
-

This cherry-like stone will fill you with joy and revival. Imagine running around through a field of sunflowers with no shoes on. Pure freedom, am I right? Wear jewellery with this stone when you are seeking love and transformation. During Reiki, you could place it anywhere on your body or just hold it in your palm. If life's got you down, get a flower agate ASAP!

Chapter Fifteen

Space Cleansing with Reiki

Every day, we are exposed to other people and their various energies, and sometimes, they may not be carrying the best of energies. When we become exposed to their toxic energies, we may end up ill or worse. Because usually, even a disease as tiny as a cold can be caused by a blocked chakra or absorbing a negative energy.

More often than not, we need to take a break from all this energy overload and take care to cleanse our auras. Inviting random and not so random people into your home leaves you susceptible to a lot of things, because they might leave pieces of their energies behind and those tiny bits of energy need to be purged.

Other reasons to cleanse your space include but are not limited to the following:

- **Psychic blood suckers.** There are some people who love dragging people down their large black hole of despair. They usually don't like empaths and look the other way when they come across one. These people can drain the life and joy out of you just like vampires, but this time, it's not your blood, it's your energy.

- **Visitors.** Your home is pretty much your temple. It is a very sacred place and should be treated as such. Personally, I don't like having a lot of people over because my home is my safe haven. It's a place I go to recharge. When people come into my home, they leave specs of their energies on my couch, floor, door handle, everywhere! And I have to cleanse for my safety and the safety of those closest to me. Your home should be your comfort zone, your sensitive place too and when you have people over, you should cleanse the environment because you want the vibe of your home to match your personal energy. Think of cleansing like adjusting the temperature of your air conditioner. I'm not saying neve have visitors. I'm saying you should take care of your safe space.

You're probably wondering how to cleanse and protect yourself because you can't avoid people until you die. Well, you can build a shield or force field around yourself with certain protective crystals in the form of house decor or jewellery.

Setting boundaries can save you a lot of trouble and stress. Think of it like drawing a line with chalk around yourself or going into a personal invincible bubble to keep from drama and stress. Boundaries are not complicated at all, not like literal walls anyway.

How to Protect Yourself with Reiki

Depending on your level in the Reiki business, you can use Reiki symbols. You could draw your symbols around you as if you are in an invisible bubble. You could say the names of the symbols at random times during your day. Draw the same symbols on top of your head, and underneath your feet.

Some people prefer the Reiki Box shaped protection. I usually recommend the egg shape, since it matches the shape of the aura. However, you can use both for different purposes whenever you like. If you are not really attuned to Reiki, or if you are still at Reiki level one, you can protect yourself by imagining white or golden light around you while meditating. I also recommend working with angels, and different Reiki colors. The color for Reiki protection is a deep violet. You can try various colors for specific protection, or to invite different angels into your home or personal space.

Cleansing Your Home

Step 1: Light your candle or candles and some sage on your altar or anywhere really. Feel free to substitute sage for incense or something else, as long as you know it's intended to cleanse. Relax, take some deep breaths before you begin. I usually state my intentions for my cleansing, and 'activate' the Reiki energy within me. Depending on what system of Reiki you use, use the form you find most comfortable. If you are not attuned to Reiki, that's okay, just pray, state your intentions for your space cleansing, and ask your angels for assistance.

Step 2: Start by spreading the sage around yourself. Go on, breathe it in, and move it all around your body, both front and back. Now you can start with the room you are currently in and try drawing the Reiki symbols on each wall of that room. You can use any symbols you like.

As you do this, be sure to speak your cleansing intentions out loud for what you want in your space. Usually, I find myself banishing negative energies from my space, and inviting angels to stay with me here in my home. I don't know about you.

Do this for all the rooms if you feel it is necessary. Depending on the frequency of your cleansings, you may only want to cleanse specific rooms. Remember to always cleanse your doorways, particularly the entrances to your home. The negative energy most likely goes through there.

Step 3: Now that you're done cleansing and sanctifying, place your sage down. Be thankful to your angels. Ask your angels & guides to keep watching and protecting you, guiding you, and fighting for you. Pray as much as you need, no time limit there. Take a deep breath in your new space, and trust me, it will feel brand new, as if you opened up a window and fresh air and positivity came through. Bask in it, love!

Whether you are into Reiki healing or empathic healing, you may be picking up energies from other people throughout the day unknowingly. Knowing how to cleanse yourself and your home is a very important survival skill.

Chapter Sixteen

KUNDALINI ENERGY

Kundalini is a dormant energy that everyone has. According to Hindu mythology, Kundalini is a serpent goddess who is sleeping at the bottom of the spine, coiled three and a half times around the sacral chakra. Her name is Kundalini Shakti, and she represents the unravelling of the divine energy, also called Shakti, the energizing essence of life itself, a living goddess who gives life to all things.

In certain situations, the Kundalini energy wakes up and begins to rise through the body, pinching and opening the chakras as it moves in its smooth, snake-like fashion. As Kundalini releases stored energies and unblocks chakras, her movement can be intense for some people and sometimes painful for others, and this almost always leads to mental states that seem totally unreal.

Situations that activate Kundalini are many and very different, but are usually triggered by the same things as extended periods of meditation, fasting, trauma yoga, stress, near death experiences, or psychedelic drugs.

Kundalini is an intense, primal force, similar to the energy found in fluids. When released, it creates a straight connection upwards between the chakras by opening the subtle channels also called **the nadi**, most especially, the central channel that moves up the spine called sushumna.

Imagine putting water through a tiny hose at a very high pressure, the end of the hose will become undulated. Same thing happens in our bodies whenever the Kundalini is awakened. Kundalini can also be as a result of the chakras connecting to each other. Theoretically speaking, when chakras are fueled with energy, they enlarge and spin on their axis. This can cause the activation of the chakra directly below or above it.

Kundalini is really just a healing force, but sometimes, the side effects of its activation can be unpleasant. This can last for years or months or minutes, it all depends. If you find yourself in the middle of unbearable Kundalini awakening symptoms, make sure to:

1. Purify the body. Stay away from tobacco, high sugar, artificial food additives, caffeine and recreational drugs. Try as much as possible to

eat healthy, especially protein. Get massages when you can and hit the gym.
2. Reduce stress.
3. Deal with your psychological issues.
4. Find help. Look for an expert on the subject.
5. Educate yourself. Study Kundalini awakening so you can better understand what is going on with you. Study Yoga and chakras too.
6. Try meditation, but stop as soon as you notice unpleasant Kundalini side effects.
7. Practice stability.

CONCLUSION

Thank you for sticking with me up until this point. Reiki is a fascinating subject with so many subtopics and links to other belief systems and religious practices.

This world is beyond the material plane and it is in our best interests to take care of our spiritual forms as much as the physical.

Reiki is an effective healing method that can be easily grasped and practised at any time. You can do your research on the subject, and figure out what works for you. I am sure there is a Reiki healing center in your area if you chose to take this path.

May the Universe guide you!

Printed in Great Britain
by Amazon